Organizational Models

Stephen P. Fitzgerald

T0341428

- Fast track route to mastering organizational models

- Covers the key areas of organizational models, from bureaucracies and infocracies to chaordic alliances and worker democracies

- Examples and lessons from some of the world's most successful businesses, including ASEA Brown Boveri, Bowstreet, Inc., Mondragon Cooperative Corporation, Softopia Japan, The Thread, and VR Techno Japan, and ideas from the smartest thinkers, including Lynda M. Applegate, Christopher Bartlett and Sumantra Goshal, Dee Hock, James Clawson, Geert Hofstede, Robert Hormats, Henry Mintzberg, Gareth Morgan, Denise M. Rousseau, and Don Tapscott

- Includes a glossary of key concepts and a comprehensive resources guide.

ORGANIZATIONS

07.07

>>EXPRESS EXEC.COM<<
essential management thinking at your fingertips

Copyright © Capstone Publishing 2002

The right of Stephen P. Fitzgerald to be identified as the author of this work has been asserted in accordance with the Copyright, Designs and Patents Act 1988

First published 2002 by
Capstone Publishing (a Wiley company)
8 Newtec Place
Magdalen Road
Oxford OX4 1RE
United Kingdom
http://www.capstoneideas.com

CIP catalogue records for this book are available from the British Library and the US Library of Congress

ISBN 1-84112-241-6

This book is printed on acid-free paper

Substantial discounts on bulk quantities of Capstone books are available to corporations, professional associations and other organizations. Please contact Capstone for more details on +44 (0)1865 798 623 or (fax) +44 (0)1865 240 941 or (e-mail) info@wiley-capstone.co.uk

Printed and bound in Great Britain by
CPI Antony Rowe, Chippenham and Eastbourne

Contents

To my mom, for everything, including her ability to lovingly organize a big family in the face of seemingly insurmountable obstacles.

Introduction to ExpressExec

ExpressExec is 3 million words of the latest management thinking compiled into 10 modules. Each module contains 10 individual titles forming a comprehensive resource of current business practice written by leading practitioners in their field. From brand management to balanced scorecard, ExpressExec enables you to grasp the key concepts behind each subject and implement the theory immediately. Each of the 100 titles is available in print and electronic formats.

Through the ExpressExec.com Website you will discover that you can access the complete resource in a number of ways:

» printed books or e-books;
» e-content – PDF or XML (for licensed syndication) adding value to an intranet or Internet site;
» a corporate e-learning/knowledge management solution providing a cost-effective platform for developing skills and sharing knowledge within an organization;
» bespoke delivery – tailored solutions to solve your need.

Why not visit www.expressexec.com and register for free key management briefings, a monthly newsletter and interactive skills checklists. Share your ideas about ExpressExec and your thoughts about business today.

Please contact elound@wiley-capstone.co.uk for more information.

Introduction to Organizational Models

Organizational models and metaphors shape our perceptions, which in turn guide our actions. Diverse new models proliferate as the pace of change continues to accelerate. Yet some believe that our social institutions, embodied in antiquated models of organization, are failing in fundamental ways. The stakes are exceedingly high at the beginning of the new millennium.

Models, models everywhere! A profusion of organizational models litters the modern business landscape, with ever more arriving at a dizzying pace. The "top of the line" in new models – those that emerge from the corporate and business school *crème de la crème*, are unveiled with all of the hoopla of the latest sports car. The business press serves as a virtual showroom for vicarious viewing of these sleekest, hottest, organizational models.

Why organizational models? Why are they important now, at the dawn of the new millennium?

Models are powerful because they shape our perceptions, and our perceptions guide our actions. Models, whether formally structured and consciously articulated, or informally imagined and subconsciously rendered (see Chapters 2 and 10), shape the way we organize and interact with all human systems, including business.

The newest models may look futuristic, but many are named like the shapes found in sugary breakfast cereals: shamrocks, stars, chaords, spiders' webs, amoebas, and so on. Of course these sound like a lot more fun than "bureaucracies" and "autocracies," that's for sure, like something we might just want to play in and have fun with. And why not? Perhaps we've reached a golden age of organizational models. Then again, perhaps we're just regressing to our collective youth.

Golden age or not, the flowering of organizational models and metaphors, and the breathtakingly rapid Internet revolution, challenge our very conceptions of what an "organization" is, what its boundaries and lifespan are, and what its structure and potential might be. The leading fringe of e-business entities in our newly-networked world blows apart our Newtonian ideas of mechanistic organizations, yet the old models still prevail in a great many businesses (see Chapter 6) – as well as inside most of our heads – and may continue to do so for quite some time.

Even though e-business pioneers and their predecessors may have left bureaucracies in the dust a few billion nanoseconds ago, your company may just be awakening from its industrial age bureaucratic slumber. Or maybe it is being re-engineered (see Chapter 8) into a more dynamic and flexible, yet still somewhat traditionally-structured, organization. Or maybe it is a thriving family business, or an autocratic entrepreneurial start-up. Given the range and diversity of business models actually in use, this book encompasses the entire spectrum of models – not just the latest and purportedly greatest.

The palette of organizational models currently in vogue changes, to a certain extent, with the times (see Chapter 3 for a brief history of the evolution of organizational models). And times have been changing, fast, throughout the waning decades of the last millennium. That trend continues to accelerate unabated. "In the first decades of the twenty-first century the velocity of economic change is likely to be even greater than it was in the supercharged 1990s," predicts Robert Hormats, vice chairman of Goldman Sachs International. "New businesses and business models will render many older ones obsolete. They, in turn, will quickly face competitive challenges. Opportunities will rapidly open and shut. Speed, adaptability, anticipation of customer needs, and skill in networking will determine success or failure. Agile and innovative Davids, individually and as part of dynamic new alliances, will challenge the traditional Goliaths with zeal, pursuing them in their own backyards and across national borders . . . Goliaths will respond by improving their own nimbleness, forging new international coalitions to pool their strengths, and forming partnerships with the very Davids who challenge them."[1] (See Chapters 6 and 7 for information on state of the art alliances and networks.)

As we hurtle towards an increasingly turbulent and uncertain future, the stakes are extraordinarily high for us all. Global visionary Dee Hock, author of *Birth of the Chaordic Age* and founder and CEO emeritus of VISA, warns: "Today, it's apparent to anyone who cares to think about it that we are in the midst of a global epidemic of institutional failure. Not just failure in the sense of collapse, such as the Soviet Union or corporate bankruptcy, but the more common and pernicious form – institutions increasingly unable to achieve the purpose for which they were created, yet continuing to expand as they devour resources, demean the human spirit and destroy the environment."[2]

It takes a moment to appreciate fully Dee Hock's words. The mind rebels: "epidemic of institutional failure" sounds so extreme and, at facevalue, inaccurate. What about the corporate stars and high-tech start-ups that adorn the covers of our business magazines? What about our tremendous scientific and technological achievements that continue apace? What about the Internet?

All true, and all perhaps to be celebrated. Yet Hock is pointing at something deeper, at something that transcends our common views of success. Our collective "success," he suggests, has served to strengthen and perpetuate global systems that are fundamentally unsustainable economically, socially, politically, environmentally, and morally. This is what he means by "institutional failure" (see Chapter 7). In this macro view, whether the stock market is up or down is immaterial. Wherever the market may happen to be, our human systems are failing to resolve the intractable issues that continue to plague our societies and our planet. Hock's point, ultimately, is "there is simply no way to govern the diversity and complexity of twenty-first century society or our enormous capacity to interfere with biospheric and genetic systems with separatist, specialist, mechanistic, seventeenth-century concepts of organization."[3]

Our conceptions of organization, our models, are powerful. They are not mere models, and they are not benign. They shape our reality, and they may ultimately hold the keys to our collective future.

Organizational Models is designed to stimulate thinking regarding the structure and design of what we have come to know as "organizations." We'll begin with a very brief overview of some of the basic definitions associated with traditional views of organizational models and structures. We'll then take a whirlwind tour of the historical evolution of organizational models, followed by the implications of e-commerce, globalization, and leading-edge thinking and practice for model-making. Three success stories are then discussed, followed by a glossary, and links to a wide variety of Web-based resources. We'll conclude with *caveats* for those considering abrupt changes to their business models, and ten guidelines for working effectively with organizational models in the twenty-first century. Each section can stand alone, and sections may be taken out of sequence and at random, to suit your particular interests and needs. It's a flexible book model.

NOTES

1 Hormats, R.D. (1999) "High velocity." *Harvard International Review*, Cambridge, MA.
2 Hock, D. (1999) *Birth of the Chaordic Age*. Berrett-Koehler, San Francisco, CA.

3 Hock, D. (November 16, 1998) "An epidemic of institutional failure: organizational development and the new millennium." Organization Development Network annual conference, New Orleans, Louisiana. (Full text available online at www.ODNetwork.org/confgallery/dee-hock.html)

Defining Organizational Models

This chapter lays the definitional foundation for the rest of the book. Model, organization, organizational model, business model, and organizational metaphor are each defined. Theoretical features of organizational structure - formalization, complexity, and centralization - are then examined. Two generic models are introduced - mechanistic and organic - that represent the range of twentieth-century thinking on organizational models. The chapter concludes with key learning points.

We begin this chapter by defining and clarifying what is meant by organizational model. Next we describe the facets of organizational structure and design that theorists use to distinguish organizational models. We conclude by using these building blocks to compare and contrast two generic models of organization that serve as a point of departure for the rest of our journey.

BASIC DEFINITIONS

Model – We hear a lot about "business models" and "organizational models," but what exactly is a *model*? Examples of models abound, and the general concept may seem straightforward enough; even so, it is important to clarify what we do and do not mean by a model. Beginning with the dictionary, *Webster's* provides several relevant definitions, including "structural design," "a pattern of something to be made," "an example for imitation or emulation," "a description or analogy used to help visualize something (as an atom) that cannot be directly observed," and "a system of postulates, data, and inferences presented as a mathematical description of an entity."[1] The word *model* also serves as a verb, with relevant definitions that include the archaic "to make into an organization (as an army, government, or parish)," as well as the more current "to plan or form after a pattern: shape," and "to construct or fashion in imitation of a particular model."[1]

Patterns, postulates, analogies, and so on really refer to abstract ideas that help us to make sense of complex phenomena that are otherwise unobservable. They are unobservable either because they are beyond the scope of our physical senses, as in an atom or a corporation, or because they do not yet exist outside of human imagination, as in an idea for a new business. Thus models not only represent what *is*, they also shape the evolution of what *might be*. They provide a road map for developing and/or understanding structure and action. A *model*, then, might be thought of as a set of interrelated concepts that represent a simplified understanding or image of key aspects of otherwise complex phenomena.

Organization – Here again, it may at first seem straightforward, but what exactly is an *organization*? Is it its people, its physical structures and locations, its products and services, its image, brand, financial statements, culture, history, leadership, or is it some combination of all of them? People come and go, physical structures and locations may change – or not even exist in today's virtual world – and so on. Thus even the concept of organization is itself amorphous at best.

Yet beneath the complexity and ambiguity, theoretical definitions of organization do not differ significantly. Chester Barnard provides perhaps the most classic and succinct definition of an organization as "a system of consciously co-ordinated activities or forces of two or more persons."[2] Organization has also been defined as a "group of people working together, under a leader, to accomplish an objective."[3] This definition does not address the issue of time – what if the group of people is replaced by a whole new group of people? What if the objective changes? In the first definition the focus is on the "system of co-ordinated activities or forces:" these may extend beyond particular individuals, goals, financial statements, and other temporary circumstances.

Given this definition, we might wonder to what extent organizations are "real," and to what extent they are "imagined." These broadly represent, in fact, two very different and yet complementary models, or images, of organizations. Imagined organizations are modeled organizations. In other words, we carry mental models of organizations that are malleable to a greater or lesser degree. It is this imagined quality, this malleability, that permits the creation and adoption of multiple images and models of the same organization. Each may provide unique insights and perspectives on a focal organization.

A more recent definition resolves the issue of continuation over time, and provides several useful additions: "An organization is a consciously co-ordinated social entity, with a relatively identifiable boundary, that functions on a relatively continuous basis to achieve a common goal or set of goals."[4]

Organizational model – A set of interrelated concepts that represent a simplified understanding or image of key aspects of an organization or organizations.

Business model – Typically regarded as a novel approach to generating a profit that shapes the structure of an organization in unique ways. The term has come into vogue in the "new," though now somewhat penitent, economy. One of the greatest business thinkers of our time, however, is less than enthused with the fad. Harvard's strategy guru Michael Porter says

> "... instead of talking in terms of strategy and competitive advantage, dot-coms and other Internet players talk about 'business models.' This seemingly innocuous shift in terminology speaks volumes. The definition of a business model is murky at best. Most often, it seems to refer to a loose conception of how a company does business and generates revenue. Generating revenue is a far cry from creating economic value, and no business model can be evaluated independently of industry structure. The business model approach to management becomes an invitation for faulty thinking and self-delusion."[5]

Of course, that approach may be viewed as a model in and of itself, competing for airtime with Porter's own well articulated and highly regarded "competitive advantage" model.

Organizational metaphor – A metaphor is a "figure of speech in which a word or phrase literally denoting one kind of object or idea [e.g., machine] is used in place of another [e.g., organization] to suggest a likeness or analogy between them (as in *drowning in money*)."[1] Good organizational metaphors transform our perceptions of organizations, thereby enabling us to see, understand, build, and/or manage them in new and surprising ways.

Organizational structure – Models often provide insights into the "structural design" of organizations. Organizational structure may be thought of as the ways in which interactions among members are patterned. This may refer to the division of the organization's work into tasks, roles, functions, and so on, as well as the co-ordination and integration of those elements through various means. Generic aspects of organizational structure include the degree and balance of the *formal* and *informal* organization (together referred to as "formalization"), differentiation and integration (which comprise "complexity"), and centralization. These aspects are defined next.

Formalization refers to the degree to which jobs, procedures, and processes are standardized and codified within the organization. This standardization may be formal or informal. *Formal organization* refers to the "official" organization, which typically appears in print in a variety of forms ranging from the organizational chart to job descriptions to policies, procedures, and operations manuals. These artefacts represent, standardize, and codify the organization as it "should" be. Of course, the degree to which these represent what actually happens within an organization is questionable. *Informal organization*, on the other hand, refers to all of the behaviors, interactions, activities, goals, objectives, and relationships that are not necessarily sanctioned by the organization. These aspects of informal organization may support and/or undermine the policies, procedures, reporting relationships, and objectives of the formal organization. They also may be overt and/or covert.

Complexity typically refers to the extent or degree of *differentiation* of tasks, roles, responsibilities, functions, etc. within an organization. There are three forms of differentiation.

» **Horizontal differentiation** is a function of the division of the organization's work into multiple jobs, tasks, roles, etc. within each level of the organization. This is also referred to as the degree of specialization.[6] Specialization may be functional, so that activities are grouped into particular jobs that various individuals may fill; or social, in terms of the specialized knowledge and skills that professionals bring to their work, and that are not easily replicated. The degree to which an organization is divided up into departments is another aspect of horizontal differentiation. Departments may be arranged by functions, products or services, clients, geographic regions, etc.

» **Vertical differentiation** refers to the height and/or depth of the organizational hierarchy. It increases as the number of levels of horizontal structure in the organization increase. It may also increase as specialization and departmentalization within an organization increase as a means of co-ordinating the increasingly differentiated horizontal structure. *Flat* organizations have low vertical differentiation, typically achieved by increasing the number of workers that report to each manager, otherwise known as increasing the "span of control."

» **Spatial differentiation** is the degree to which an organization's people, activities, and locations are geographically dispersed.

It may be thought of as extending an organization's horizontal and/or vertical differentiation by separating activities, functions, departments, units, etc. in different geographic locations.

Complexity increases as an organization becomes more horizontally, vertically, and spatially differentiated. As complexity increases, the need for coordination, communication, and control mechanisms also increases to ensure that highly differentiated functions, departments, units, people, etc. work effectively together toward achieving organizational objectives.

Centralization is typically thought of as the degree to which decision-making is concentrated at a single point in the organization. Stephen Robbins offers this expanded definition of centralization: "the degree to which the formal authority to make discretionary choices is concentrated in an individual, unit, or level (usually high in the organization), thus permitting employees (usually low in the organization) minimum input into their work."[4] Thus centralization refers to the degree to which decision-making authority is concentrated – or dispersed – among individuals, units, or levels within the organization.

Systems – Organizational systems range from closed to open.

Closed system represents the view that a natural or social system is largely self-contained, with boundaries that are relatively impervious to the environments that surround it, and to changes that occur in those environments.

Open system is often referred to as a systems perspective, in which a natural or social system is viewed as being highly dependent upon the environments in which it is immersed, and constantly interacting with those environments through its permeable boundaries.

A TALE OF TWO MODELS

These building blocks of organizational structure may be used to distinguish various models of organization. For example, "mechanistic" and "organic" have been identified as two prototypical models of organization based on distinct structural configurations.[7] A mechanistic organization is viewed as being a closed system that is complex vertically and horizontally, highly formalized, standardized, and centralized, with narrow spans of control, whereas an organic organization is conceived of as an open system that is low in vertical and horizontal complexity, formalization, and standardization, and highly decentralized with broad spans of control. These two extremes largely bracket twentieth-century thinking on organizational models.

KEY LEARNING POINTS

» **Model** – a set of interrelated concepts that represent a simplified understanding or image of key aspects of otherwise complex phenomena.
» **Organization** – "a consciously co-ordinated social entity, with a relatively identifiable boundary, that functions on a relatively continuous basis to achieve a common goal or set of goals."[4]
» **Organizational model** – a set of interrelated concepts that represent a simplified understanding or image of key aspects of an organization or organizations.
» **Business model** – a novel approach to generating a profit that shapes the structure of an organization in unique ways.
» **Organizational structure** – ways in which interactions among members are patterned. Includes formalization, centralization, and complexity.
» **Closed vs. open systems** – refers to perceptions of a system as being either self-contained or dependent upon its environment.
» **Mechanistic vs. organic models** – bracket twentieth-century thinking on organizational models.

NOTES

1 *Webster's Ninth New Collegiate Dictionary* (1991) Merriam-Webster Inc., Springfield, MA.
2 Barnard, C.I. (1938) *The Functions of the Executive*. Harvard University Press, Cambridge, MA.
3 Tosi, H.L. (1975) *Theories of Organization*. St Clair Press, Chicago.
4 Robbins, S.P. (1990) *Organization Theory, Structure, Design, and Applications*, 3rd edn. Prentice Hall, Englewood Cliffs, NJ.

5 Porter, M.E. (2001) "Strategy and the Internet." *Harvard Business Review*, March.

6 Daft, R.L. (1992) *Organization Theory and Design*, 4th edn. West, St Paul, MN.

7 Anthony, W., Gales, L., & Hodge, B. (1996) *Organization Theory: A Strategic Approach*. Prentice Hall, Englewood Cliffs, NJ. (based on the work of Burns & Stalker, 1961).

The Evolution of Organizational Models

Hierarchical models of organization are several millennia old. Religious entities served as primary organizational models for many centuries. During the twentieth century the trend was from mechanistic, closed-system, bureaucratic models, toward organic, open-system, autocratic models. There has been a flowering of organizational models and metaphors in recent decades. Key models and metaphors are introduced.

» A bit of ancient history:
  » religious organizations.
» Organizational models of the twentieth century:
  » major phases;
  » Mintzberg's five "natural configurations";
  » other models.
» Key learning points.

The pursuit of the perfect means of organizing a business has taken managers through a bewildering array of possible models and structures. Today, new organizational forms emerge with regularity, while many organizations continue to cling tenaciously to traditional models.

A BIT OF ANCIENT HISTORY

In the beginning there was hierarchy. A Greek called Dionysios the Areopagite purportedly introduced the concept of hierarchy some 1500 years ago. The word *hierarchy* literally means "rule by the sacred." Dionysios – not the mythological wine god, that was Dionysus – said that the heavens were hierarchically organized. The source of this knowledge is lost in the mists of time. He also argued that this celestial structure had exactly nine levels. This concept survived into the Christian era: God was considered to be the CEO; the archangels acting as the top-management team, and Jesus Christ in a staff position to the right of God. According to the theory, hell is also hierarchically organized – again with nine layers. The entire structure is turned upside down, however, with purgatory as the prime motivator to "climb" the ladder. Medieval painters had a field day with this view of the universe – humans inhabit a central open plan office, looking up to nine levels, called "spheres," which become progressively difficult to achieve, and looking down into the prospect of nine basement levels which are all too easy to achieve!

The Egyptians understand all too well the hell-like possibilities of hierarchy. The Mugama ("Uniting") Central Government Complex office was for decades "the most feared and hated structure in Egypt and the evolutionary product of millennia of bureaucracy on the shores of the Nile."[1] Just how feared and hated? Enough to prompt twelve people to jump from the foreboding structure's windows and balconies to their deaths in the courtyard below.

Political sociologist Saad Eddin Ibrahim explains: "The Mugama is to Egypt generally a symbol of 4000 years of bureaucracy, and for the average Egyptian, it means all that is negative about the bureaucracy: routine, slow paperwork, complicated paperwork, a lot of signatures, impersonality."[1] four thousand years is plenty of time to perfect an organizational model, and of course Dionysios the Areopagite may have to battle it out with the Pharoahs to lay claim to the origins of the hierarchical model. That model later influenced, and was intricately elaborated and refined by, Egypt's French, Turkish and British occupiers.[1]

Suffice it to say that the hierarchic, bureaucratic model of organization had been discovered and implemented long before the dawn of the Industrial Revolution.

More recently, the Incas expanded their North American Empire during the fifteenth century. At their peak, the Incas controlled six million people spread over a huge area covering parts of modern Peru, Ecuador, Chile, Bolivia, and Argentina. They spoke many different languages and dialects. Managing them and their lands was a bit more challenging than managing a distant subsidiary.

The Incas recognized that communication, logistics, and administration are vital in any large, dispersed organization. Their resulting organizational model involved a network of administrative centers and warehouses for food, thousands of miles of roads (astonishing given the fact that they had no vehicles with wheels), and a highly standardized system of administration based on units of ten that was the forerunner of the modern decimal system. The system worked, but briefly: the Inca empire functioned for only 100 years.

RELIGIOUS ORGANIZATIONS

Christian religious organizations were *the* organizational models for many centuries in the West, and many structural and technological innovations were introduced through them over time. For example, the Cistercians, part of the Benedictine order of monks, were established in 1098 with a mission to escape the excesses of worldliness and live "remote from the habitation of man." St Bernard of Clairvaux (1090–1153) entered the Cistercian monastery of Cîteaux in 1112 and provided dynamic leadership. In addition to writing exhaustively (400 epistles, 340 sermons, various treatises, and a life of St Malachy), St Bernard decided that the order needed to become efficient in fending for itself, and he founded more than 70 monasteries. As a result, the order embraced the latest in technology. Monasteries were remote from man but they were near to streams - these were used to provide power (the water-wheel was a relatively recent, but vital discovery), running water, and a means of sewage disposal. "These monasteries were, in reality, the best organized factories the world had ever seen," says John Lienhard of the University of Houston. "They were versatile and diversified."

The Society of Jesus (the Jesuits) was founded in 1540 by Ignatius de Loyola. According to Peter Drucker, it became "the most successful staff organization in the world," based an organizational model that emphasized practical work rather than contemplation. Then of course there is the hierarchy of the Roman Catholic Church – low on layers (five, beginning with the Pope and extending down to cardinals, archbishops, bishops, and parish priests), but top-heavy on authority, with Rome presiding over its 400,000 priests and the millions of believers that they minister to. Now *that's* a high degree of centralization! Of course the threat of eternal damnation may serve as a significant deterrent against insurrection or hostile takeover attempts. The second Vatican Council (1962–65) called by Pope John XXIII launched one of the biggest change management programs in history. It altered the shape of the Catholic Church – a low hierarchy management model that has stood the test of time.

ORGANIZATIONAL MODELS OF THE TWENTIETH CENTURY

The last century gave birth to a cornucopia of academic disciplines related to management and organizations, and along with it, a similar bounty of organizational models. Nevertheless, devotion to the hierarchical ideal, honed to perfection over the past few millennia, does not quickly evaporate, regardless of the exhortations of modern business thinkers. For example, in a 1992–93 survey, Harvard's Lynda Applegate asked 500 managers of small to large companies world-wide to compare their organizations to the characteristics of hierarchies and the sorts of newer models heralded in the business press.[2] The majority of managers responded that their organizations continued to be traditionally structured with a full complement of hierarchical accoutrements. Still, the managers believed that within five years their organizations would – and should – look like the flatter, decentralized, informal, networked sorts of models that the management gurus were selling. Time, of course, will tell.

Overall, however, the general trend in organizational models during the last century has been from traditional, mechanistic, bureaucratic forms, to non-traditional, organic, "adhocratic" forms (see below). Traditional systems are viewed as closed systems (i.e. isolated from their environments) that exhibit high levels of formalization, standardization, and rigidity, and that tend to be deterministic, normative, and conservative. Adhocracies, on the other hand, are viewed as open systems characterized by informality, flexibility, dynamism, ambiguity, and that tend to be more loosely structured, contingency oriented, and opportunistic.

MAJOR PHASES

The field of Organizational Theory – the academic discipline that studies organizational models and structures – went through four major phases during the last century. The first 30 years were heavily influenced by the hierarchical inheritance of history, the rapid development of factories as an outgrowth of the industrial revolution, and by the contributions of Frederick Taylor, Henri Fayol, Max Weber, and Ralph Davis.[3]

Taylor, an American mechanical engineer, published the highly influential *Principles of Scientific Management* in 1911. He applied scientific tools to the study of the rapidly evolving phenomena of manufacturing organizations. Taylor believed that there was "one best way" to perform a job, and that jobs should be engineered to those specifications. Thus Taylor's "scientific management" was in fact mechanistic management. Build and run the organization as a finely-tuned machine. In a machine, the parts – the workers – are interchangeable.

Frenchman Henri Fayol offered 14 "universal" principles of organization based upon his extensive experience as an executive. Some of the those principles are that work becomes more efficient when divided into separate tasks and jobs, communications should flow from top to bottom of the hierarchy along what Fayol called the "scalar chain," decision-making should be centralized to the optimal degree (for *centralization* – see Chapter 2), managers must have authority commensurate with their level of responsibility, and they must also treat their subordinates equitably.

German sociologist Max Weber codified bureaucracy as an ideal organizational model. Core attributes of Weber's bureaucracy include division of labor (like Fayol's first principle), power and authority vested in hierarchically arranged offices/positions and not in individuals (i.e. impersonal structure), and high formalization. Though bureaucracy is not synonymous with hierarchy, the terms are related – a bureaucratic model is hierarchical by definition – and often used interchangeably. The model was, and continues to be, highly influential in structuring large organizations.

During these first three decades of the last century, organizations were conceived as closed (i.e. self-contained), rational, mechanistic systems. The second phase of the last century spanned from roughly 1930 through the early 1960s. During this time, organizations continued to be viewed as closed systems, but Elton Mayo's famous Hawthorne Studies launched the Human Relations Movement, and with it the recognition that organizations are social – not just mechanical – systems. Chester Barnard, based upon his extensive experience with AT&T, integrated the ideas inherent in the mechanical and social models into a view of organizations as being co-operative systems.[4]

In 1960, Douglas McGregor introduced his now famous "Theory X/Theory Y" dichotomised view of workers as being either inherently work-aversive, responsibility-shirking, security-seeking, and ambition-less (Theory X), or as creative, self-directed, and responsibility-seeking people who enjoy work as a natural and vital part of life (Theory Y). McGregor's model has been highly influential in promoting participative management systems and structures based on Theory Y principles. Ouchi and Jaeger later introduced a "Theory Z" model of organizations (see Chapter 5).

In 1966, management visionary Warren Bennis heralded the death of bureaucracy. He "predicted that the ponderous decision-making and functional divisions of the industrial age bureaucracy would render them obsolete."[5] Decentralization and democratic decision-making, and authority based on expertise rather than hierarchical position, were seen as the hallmarks of the emerging "autocratic" organizational model as stable industry environments were increasingly plowed under by the accelerating churn of technological change.

The third major phase of the past century began in the 1960s and continued through the mid 1970s. Developments in the natural sciences and systems theory influenced organizational theorists and changed forever the view of organizations as closed systems. From that point forward, organizations were viewed as open systems that are highly dependent upon the environments in which they operate. Daniel Katz and Robert Kahn introduced the idea that organizations need to adapt to their environments in order to survive.[6] This led to contingency approaches to organizational models, where choosing the "right" model for a particular organization is based on a rational assessment of the relative stability of the environments in which it operates. During this period the appropriate structure for an organization also came to be seen as being contingent upon its size and technology.

A diversity of organizational models flowered in the fourth phase during the last quarter century. All are rooted in an open systems view. They shift focus toward more adaptive models that recognize and incorporate the dynamics of organizational power and politics. Professor Jeffrey Pfeffer proposed that organizational structures are not established merely as the result of rational processes, but rather as a function of the self-serving political aims of those with power in the organization.

MINTZBERG'S FIVE "NATURAL CONFIGURATIONS"

At the dawn of the power-politics phase, Henry Mintzberg integrated the prior research on contingency approaches into a coherent and influential contingency model of organizational structure.[7] He identified five configurations: simple structure, machine bureaucracy, professional bureaucracy, divisionalised form, and adhocracy.

» **Simple structures** are characteristic of the early, entrepreneurial years of most organizations. According to Mintzberg[7] "the heyday of the simple structure probably occurred during the period of the great American trusts, late in the nineteenth century". Simple structures are low on formalization, and decision-making is highly centralized in the founder/entrepreneur/owner. This enables them to remain flexible in order to respond quickly to the dynamic and sometimes hostile environments in which they typically operate.

» **Machine bureaucracies** are, of course, a by-product of industrialization. They are hierarchic, highly standardized, and formalized to enable effective co-ordination of highly specialized, low-skilled workers, and with a technostructure as the central focus of the organization (as in manufacturing). This model adapts well in simple, stable environments – in other words, during days gone by. Mintzberg notes that many young companies fail because their entrepreneurial founders are unable to incorporate bureaucratic structures when their organizations grow beyond the capacity of simple structures.

» **Professional bureaucracies** are based on standardized skill sets rather than tasks, jobs, or work processes as in machine bureaucracies. Accounting and law firms, hospitals, and universities often develop according to this model. There is a split between the professional and administrative staff, which is relatively large. This leads to the development of parallel hierarchies, "one democratic with bottom-up power for the professionals, and a second autocratic with top-down control for the support staff".[7] Mintzberg notes that this model emerged mid-twentieth century, and is increasingly popular due to the high level of autonomy enjoyed by those considered to be "professionals".

» **Divisionalized form** is the result of the diversification of an organization's product lines. It is not a "pure" form, in that each division has its own structure – typically based on the machine bureaucracy model due to the need for standardization of outputs across divisions. It is characteristic of the structure of large corporations.

When Alfred P. Sloan took over the top job at General Motors in the 1920s, GM had been built up through the regular and apparently random acquisition of small companies. Sloan organized the company into eight divisions – five car divisions and three component divisions. Each of the units was made responsible for all its commercial operations, with its own engineering, production, and sales departments, but was supervised by a central staff responsible for overall policy and finance.

This marked the invention of the divisionalized organization. The multi-divisional form enabled Sloan to utilize the company's size without making it cumbersome. "The multi-divisional organization was perhaps the single most important administrative innovation that helped companies grow in size and diversity far beyond the limits of the functional organization it replaced," say contemporary thinkers Sumantra Ghoshal and Christopher Bartlett.

Sloan's innovation required a continuous balancing act, but it worked. By 1925, with its new organization and commitment to annual changes in its automotive models, GM had overtaken Ford, which continued to persist with its faithful old Model T. However, the deficiencies of Sloan's model gradually became apparent. The decentralized structure built up by Sloan revolved around a reporting and committee infrastructure that eventually became unwieldy. As time went by, more and more committees were set up. Stringent targets and narrow measures of success stultified initiative. By the end of the 1960s the delicate balance between centralization and decentralization, which Sloan had brilliantly maintained, was lost. Finance emerged as the dominant function, and GM became paralyzed by what had once made it great.

» **Adhocracy** is a highly flexible, adaptive, informal, organic model of organization. Management visionary Warren Bennis first introduced the concept of adhocracy in the 1960s. This form is traditionally found in industries like aerospace and film-making that depend upon transient teams of experts that come together to complete large-scale projects. However, the characteristics of adhocracies are for the most part the same as those lauded by management gurus today. Adhocracies are particularly well-suited for innovation in highly complex, dynamic environments. They are characterized by large numbers of managers with narrow spans of control over aspects of projects and small teams of highly specialized experts. However, power shifts fluidly according to the particular knowledge or expertise needed at any given moment. The adhocratic form has been powerfully enabled by the rapid ubiquity of network technologies and the rapid development of knowledge workers.

OTHER MODELS

The matrix

No, not the movie, and not quite an alternative reality. Really a variation on the multi-divisional model, matrix management is an organizational structure which is not based on a simple chain of command, but where individuals report to two (or more) bosses.

This sort of structure was adopted by many multinational companies. As much as anything, matrix management was an attempt to clarify responsibilities and reporting lines in large companies with operations in more than one national market.

Under a typical matrix management system, a marketing manager in, say, Germany reports ultimately to a boss in that country, but also to the head of the marketing function back in the company's home country. The two reporting lines are the two sides to the matrix, which has a geographical and a functional axis.

As a theoretical model, the matrix is a neat solution to the complexity of large companies. However, in reality, power cannot be evenly balanced, and conflicts inevitably arise. When you add in additional complexity such as cross-functional reporting lines in project teams or start-up operations, the poor marketing manager can end up trying to please several different bosses at the same time.

The real question with a matrix structure is where does the power lie? Is it with the national manager, or is it with the function head back at HQ? Attempts to resolve these sorts of problems have been largely a case of fudging the decision-making structure to suit the circumstance. Many multinationals continue to operate as matrix management structures simply because they have not come up with a better model.

Family business

Throughout the twentieth century, the predominant corporate myth was that big was good. From Henry Ford to Michael Eisner, Alfred P. Sloan to Jack Welch, size has been considered all-important. Bravado, of a peculiarly male kind, has dominated. The current fashion for bigger and bigger mergers is just the latest manifestation of this obsession. We may accept that quantity is not quality in virtually every other area, but in business organizations the two remain hopelessly intertwined and confused.

The trouble is that expert after expert has pointed out that most people are not very creative in groups of 100,000, 10,000, 1000, or even 500. People tend to be at their most creative in small teams. On the Savannah Plain 200,000 years ago, clans appeared to have had a maximum of around 150 members.[8] Nigel Nicholson of London Business School points to "the persistent strength of small to mid-size family businesses throughout history. These companies, typically having no more than 150 members, remain the predominant model the world over, accounting for approximately 60 percent of all employment."

THE FLOWERING OF ORGANIZATIONAL METAPHORS

Whether or not the bureaucratic model is destined to become a relic of history, there has been a flowering of alternatives. In his groundbreaking, now classic, work, Gareth Morgan refers to them as "Images of Organization."[9] The brilliance of Morgan's work is the clarity with which he elucidates the metaphors we *live* – they do not simply describe organizational reality, they frame how we perceive it, interact with it, and even co-create it. Those metaphors range from the familiar machine, organism, brain, culture, and political systems models to the more esoteric "psychic prisons," "flux and transformation," and the eternally endearing "instruments of domination" models.

YET MORE MODELS

This chapter barely scratches the surface of the surfeit of organizational models that have been proposed by management thinkers and/or actually tried in organizations during the last quarter century. More recent innovations include:

» the shamrock organization;
» membership communities;
» the star;
» the boundaryless organization;
» the amoeba;
» the chemical soup organization (i.e. project teams);

» the virtual or hollowed-out organization;
» numerous e-business models;
» incubators;
» alliances and networks; and
» chaordic alliances.

And there are still more. Some are featured in the next three chapters, and the remainder are briefly covered in the glossary in Chapter 8.

KEY LEARNING POINTS

» According to Dionysios the Areopagite, heaven and hell are hierarchically organized. Who are we to question hierarchy?
» Christian religious organizations were *the* model for centuries in the West.
» Four phases of organizational theory and models in the twentieth century:
  » Hierarchy and bureaucracy – closed, rational systems;
  » Organizations as closed, co-operative social-mechanical systems;
  » Open systems dependent on their environments – contingency;
  » Diversity of open systems models – power and politics.
» Mintzberg's five "natural configurations":
  » simple structures – early entrepreneurial organizations;
  » machine bureaucracies – hierarchical and standardized;
  » professional bureaucracies – standardized skill sets;
  » divisionalized form – subsidiary form of large corporations;
  » "adhocracy" – highly flexible, adaptive, informal, organic model.
» The matrix – dual reporting structure – geographic × function;
» Family business – predominant model world-wide, most with less than 150 members, account for around 60% of all employment;
» Organizational metaphors – range from "machines," "organisms," and "brains," to "psychic prisons" and the ever-popular "instruments of domination."

NOTES

1 Murphy, K. (1993) "Woe awaits in tower of babble." *Los Angeles Times*, May 24.

2 Applegate, L.M. (1993) *Business Transformation Self-assessment: Summary of Findings, 1992-93* Case no. 194-013, Harvard Business School, Boston, MA.

3 Robbins, S.P. (1990) *Organization Theory, Structure, Design, and Application*, 3rd edn. Prentice Hall, Englewood Cliffs, NJ.

4 Barnard, C.I. (1938) *The Functions of the Executive*. Harvard University Press, Cambridge, MA.

5 Clawson, J. (2000) "The new infocracies: implications for leadership." *Ivey Business Journal*, May/June [London].

6 Katz, D. & Kahn, R. (1966) *The Social Psychology of Organizations*. John Wiley, New York.

7 Mintzberg, H. (1981) "Organization design: fashion or fit?" *Harvard Business Review*, January/February (based on his 1979 book *The Structuring of Organizations*, Prentice-Hall, NJ).

8 Nicholson, N. (1998) "How hardwired is human behavior?" *Harvard Business Review*, July/August

9 Morgan, G. (1986) *Images of Organization*. Sage, Beverly Hills, CA.

The E-Dimension of Organizational Models

The Internet is having a profound impact on organizational models, and our very conceptions of what constitutes an "organization." Business models have become the hot e-business buzzword, and a sampling of those models is presented. Business webs – a rapidly-emerging model – facilitate and expedite the disaggregation of vertically-integrated organizational structures. Not long ago, "incubator" models were all the rage – until the tech markets toppled. The future of incubators is explored, featuring the case of a public/private partnership in Japan.

» From bureaucracies to "infocracies."
» From organizational models to business models.
» Business webs.
» Fasten your seatbelts – we're dismantling organizations.
» Incubators – poorly-hatched models?
» Best practice: a "sweet" incubator in Japan.
» Business models: magic bullet?
» Key learning points.

The e-dimension has revolutionized – or at the very least significantly infiltrated – every aspect of modern life, including models of organization. The ubiquity of electronic exchange systems and media, and the rapid evolution of networking technologies associated with them, is accelerating the transition away from mechanistic models of organization toward more organic network forms. At the heart of this transition is the birth of the information age and its implications for organizational models.

FROM BUREAUCRACIES TO "INFOCRACIES"

During the past half-century, a major transition has been affecting every aspect of organizations and their models. Stable industry environments were increasingly plowed under by the accelerating churn of technological change, the workforce became highly educated, natural and manufacturing resources became commoditized, and information rose to primacy as the key resource at the center of organizational life. We are now immersed in the information age, and James Clawson identifies it as a major historical shift from bureaucracy to what he calls "infocracy."[1]

In a bureaucracy, power and authority are vested in offices and positions, not individuals. Laws and policies take precedence over personal judgment. In an infocracy, data is at the core, and it overrides both policies and personal judgment. Authority is vested in those who interpret the data. As Clawson explains, power "migrates to whoever is closest to the key challenges facing the organization at any given time and who has access to the relevant data for making the appropriate decision."[1] The entire structure of the organization becomes centered around and built upon information systems.

Interestingly, Clawson notes that infocracies "share some characteristics of the bureaucracies they are replacing. They have not entirely abandoned hierarchy, and they have maintained certain internal policies, procedures and measurement systems in the interest of control and order. Leadership continues to be important."[1] The *shape* of infocracies is considerably different however – flatter, more fluid, organic, and network-like. Clawson goes on to identify 10 implications for leadership in infocracies, including moving away from the command-and-control style associated with bureaucracies, and toward data-based persuasion. The transition to infocracies has generated a profusion of new models, and a shift in focus from "organizational" to "business" models.

FROM ORGANIZATIONAL MODELS TO BUSINESS MODELS

Everywhere today you read about business models, yet it is seldom clear what is meant by the term in general. And little seems to relate to the traditional structural elements associated with the study of organizational models (e.g. formalization, complexity – see Chapter 2). That may be due, in part, to the rising prominence of the field of business strategy over the past two decades. Business models derive primarily from that field, whereas traditional organizational models have emerged from multiple arenas, with a focus of study in organizational theory. Thus there has been a shift in emphasis from structural aspects in the foreground of organizational models to strategic elements in the foreground of business models.

The wired world spits out new business models faster than you can say B2B. But before embarking on a brief exploration of this dynamic new world, it is important first to clarify what business models are and, for purposes of this text, how they relate to older ideas of organizational models, if at all.

Michael Rappa, a professor at North Carolina State University and creator of the free online course *Managing the Digital Enterprise* (used by over 150 universities world-wide, and by several corporations – see Chapter 9 for details), defines a business model as a "method of doing business by which a company can sustain itself – that is, generate revenue. The business model spells out how a company makes money by specifying where it is positioned in the value chain."[2] He says that while the wired world will certainly spawn entirely new business models, "the Web is also likely to reinvent tried-and-true models. Auctions are a perfect example. One of the oldest business models, auctions have been widely used throughout the world to set prices for such items as agricultural commodities, financial instruments, and unique items like fine art and antiquities. Companies like eBay have popularized the auction model and broadened the application on the Web to a wide array of goods and services."[2]

Henry Chesbrough and Richard S. Rosenbloom of Harvard Business School clarify the features of a business model in the following operational definition:

> "The functions of a business model are to:
> » articulate the value proposition, that is, the value created for users by the offering based on the technology;
> » identify a market segment, that is, the users to whom the technology is useful and for what purpose;
> » define the structure of the value chain within the firm required to create and distribute the offering;
> » estimate the cost structure and profit potential of producing the offering, given the value proposition and value chain structure chosen;
> » describe the position of the firm within the value network linking suppliers and customers, including identification of potential complementors and competitors; and
> » formulate the competitive strategy by which the innovating firm will gain and hold advantage over rivals."[3]

Professor Lynda M. Applegate, also of Harvard, has published extensively on the impact of information technologies on organizational models, structures, and strategies, with 100 cases and articles available online at Harvard Business School Publishing (www.hbsp.harvard.edu, see Chapter 9 for additional information). Applegate bridges approaches to industrial age models with those of the information age. In her latest update on e-business models, she says, "as you review the business model framework, it is important to recognize that the components and relationships depicted here are not new. Indeed, this basic approach has been used for decades to analyze a variety of industrial business models. What is new are the business rules and assumptions that form the *mental models* that, in turn, guide how we make decisions and take actions."[4]

Applegate compares and contrasts industrial and information age organizational models.[4] Key differences include all of those structural aspects represented in the shift from mechanistic to organic models (see Chapter 2), and much more. For example, the center of market power in the value chain (i.e. suppliers, producers, distributors, customers) has shifted from producers in the industrial age to networked distributors like AOL-Time Warner in the information age. There has also been a major shift from proprietary to shared digital business infrastructure, which enables "new entrants and established firms to create and exploit *network* economies of scale and scope."[4]

2In Applegate's conceptualization, the building blocks of business models include the business concept (e.g. market opportunity, strategy), capabilities (e.g. infrastructure, operating, and management models), and value (e.g. benefits to all stakeholders and to the organization). Using these building blocks, Applegate distinguishes two broad categories of e-business models – businesses that are "built on" the Internet, and those that develop and provide the network infrastructure. She identifies three generic e-business models within each category: *Producers* (e.g. General Motors), *Focused Distributors* (e.g. Drugstore.com), and *Portals* in the "built on the Internet" category, and *Infrastructure Producers* (e.g. Oracle.com), *Distributors* (e.g. NECX), and *Portals* (e.g. Sales.com) in the "infrastructure provider" category. Finally, each of these sub-categories itself contains several distinct models. For example, Applegate describes five different Focused Distributor e-business models: *Retailers* (e.g. Amazon.com), *Marketplaces* (e.g. E-Loan), *Infomediaries* (e.g. Office.com), *Exchanges* (e.g. eBay.com), and *Aggregators* (e.g. Quicken Investing). (The chapter contains many tables and graphics that make it easy to distinguish the features of the different models).

These are by no means the only e-business models that have been created. For example, Michael Rappa offers nine generic e-business models: Brokerage, Advertising, Infomediary, Merchant, Manufacturer, Affiliate, Community, Subscription, and Utility. Of course several distinct models can be identified within most of these generic forms. For example, Rappa describes 12 different types of brokerage models.

The profusion of e-business models creates the illusion that each firm pursues only one model. However, Applegate clearly shows that the boundaries are blurring, and that today's "e-businesses are built by artfully combining a variety of business models ... By incorporating multiple business models that generate separate streams off of the same infrastructure, a network of businesses can more efficiently use resources, more effectively meet customer needs for integrated solutions, and drive additional value from the same level of investment''. Networks of online businesses represent the latest e-business model, the Business Web (b-web).

BUSINESS WEBS

The hottest business/organizational model

And so they are as of this writing in Fall 2001, though of course given the speed of change they may be *passé* by the time of publication. That is unlikely, however. Business webs integrate many of the trends that have been discussed to date. They are enabled not merely by the presence of the Internet and intranets, but by the development of new technologies that provide a quantum leap in the speed and ease with which distinct organizations and individuals, and the myriad information systems that they have independently developed, can be integrated to achieve common objectives. Those objectives may be fleeting or longer-term.

Although the Internet itself establishes the potential for b-webs, that potential has been impeded by the challenges of rapid integration across multiple information systems designed around different standards. However, those challenges are rapidly being overcome with the creation of dynamic new integrative solutions. Bowstreet, Inc. is at the leading edge of creating those solutions. Bowstreet automates – yes *automates* – the design and assembly of composite web applications – key to facilitating the rapid proliferation of b-webs. Their solutions promote the use and re-use of components across related families of applications, thereby enabling greater efficiency in successive development efforts. Further, this enables IT specialists to give users an unprecedented ability to tailor with ease the way their applications behave in order to meet their unique needs, thereby freeing IT specialists to focus on more pressing tasks. It enables e-businesses to coalesce rapidly to form a b-web in order to take advantage of short- and/or long-range market opportunities (see Chapter 7 for a success story, The Thread, involving Bowstreet technology).

Fasten your seatbelts – we're dismantling organizations

Business webs reveal the full implications of the transition from mechanistic to organic models of organization that has been accelerating over the past several decades. B-webs involve nothing short of the dismantling of vertically-integrated organizational structures. Over time, they will obviate the need for – and the considerable costs associated with the maintenance of – those structures. Those structures are what we typically think of when we think of *organization*.

The potential repercussions are vast. Don Tapscott (www.dontapscott.com) is chairman of Digital 4Sight (a Toronto research institute), and a leading international expert and author of eight books on business models and organizational strategy in the digital age.[5] Tapscott and his colleagues identify five generic b-web models: *agora* (or market center, e.g. eBay), *aggregation* (e.g. E-Trade), *value chain* (e.g. Cisco), *alliance* (e.g. software development for Palm Pilot), and *distributive network* (e.g. FedEx, and the Internet itself).[5] But, more importantly, the authors provide rich insight into the tremendous impact that the emergence of b-webs may have. "All sectors of the economy will experience the benefits of b-webs," says Tapscott, "since they will effectively replace the corporation as the foundation for wealth creation in the digital economy."[6]

In this brave new networked world, customers become integrated into the b-web as co-creators of products and services. Further, Tapscott notes "products are becoming experiences. The old industrial approaches to product definition and product marketing die. Dell is a great example of understanding the power of b-webs. Dell's Web-based customer integration initiatives began with its Premiere Pages, which customize options, pricing, and policies for each individual customer."[6]

Where to begin? "Each business must first be prepared to disaggregate all of its functional elements," says Newt Barrett in his review of *Digital Capital* for businessnewsnow.com[7] (which itself is based on an aggregator b-web model). [Note: this trend is a natural extension of outsourcing non-core business functions. See "virtual" and "hollow" organizational models in Chapter 8 for additional information.] "Then, by starting with the customer as the focal point and with the Internet as a core enabler," Newt continues, "it must reaggregate functionality – keeping for itself only those processes that cannot be allocated to other providers more efficiently ... In the end, each partner will concentrate on what it does best. The net result is that superb return on capital can be expected when b-webs operate effectively. Revenue growth can be exponential while costs show modest linear growth."

Make no mistake. Whether or not b-webs have the level of impact that Tapscott and his collaborators prophesy, they most likely will generate, and indeed already are generating, dynamic new business models that challenge our most fundamental images of organizations.

Incubators: poorly hatched models?

Just before the demise of the high-tech markets, "incubators" had quickly become *the* hot business model for launching e-businesses. Riding on the dot-com tidal wave, incubators quickly became all the rage, however, "the incubator age now has been declared dead before it ever really got started."[8] Incubators were essentially investment vehicles for nurturing high-tech start-ups. The model was based on investors setting up a firm that would typically provide a full range of support services (e.g. physical space, equipment, consulting, and legal services) to fledgling e-businesses in exchange for equity in those businesses.

idealab! Inc., based in Pasadena and Palo Alto, California, was once one of the brightest stars in the dazzling incubator skies. It is known for launching Internet retailers like eToys.com. But it, like so many others, turned out to be a shooting star.

High-tech centers around the world raced to establish incubators. For example, the number of European incubators rocketed from about three in 1999 to an estimated 200 or more by June 2000. The UK, in particular, was a hotbed of home-grown incubator activity, with companies such as Brainspark, NewMedia Spark and Ideas Hub. Other incubator hotspots included Germany, France, Sweden, and the Netherlands. The names behind some of the leading European incubators were significant. They included the French businessman Bernard Arnault, whose Internet investment vehicle Europ@web was modeled on the US CMGI Group, a publicly listed network.

But when the e-business market took a nosedive, the flaws in the model became woefully apparent. "It's harsh, but fair, to say that a large number of the new breed of European [and American] incubators and accelerators are now in a mess. Some have returned funds to their investors, others have dropped out of view taking significant losses with them and others have stopped investing."[8]

Some incubators tried to reinvent themselves by calling themselves "accelerators," without substantive changes to the underlying business model. However, although many incubators/accelerators seem to have died, the need that they filled remains. Some seed-stage investment companies are rethinking their business models based on what they have learned from the rapid demise of so many incubators.

One such company is AV Labs, based in Austin, Texas. According to Rob Adams, AV Labs' managing director, "the firm does not have a huge incubator-like development team in place. Instead its portfolio companies can decide to use third-party service providers. While portfolio companies can move into AV Labs' facility, it is not a requirement and the companies themselves manage their own resources, deciding how they want to spend their capital."[8] In addition, unlike incubators, once AV Labs has provided first-round funding for one of its portfolio companies, it will not invest subsequent funds in it until that company generates a commitment for additional funding from another party. Observers anticipate a consolidation among seed-money companies during the down market, and while some incubators will no doubt pass muster and continue, new models will also emerge over time.

A "SWEET" INCUBATOR IN JAPAN

While most eyes have been turned toward the rise, fall, consolidation, and remodelling of private high-tech incubators in the US and Europe, Japan has been quietly creating a dynamic duo of incubators in the midst of its Sweet Valley Project (www.sweetvalley.jp/e_index.htm). Located on a wide plain that spans the south of Japan's Gifu Prefecture, between Tokyo and Osaka in the center of the country, Sweet Valley is surrounded by natural beauty as well as academic institutions and commercial research centers that help make it a truly sweet spot for nurturing the formation of a concentration of IT industries.

Gifu aspires to become Japan's Silicon Valley and has been developing research centers and other support institutions there (such as the Institute of Manufacturing and Information Technologies) for almost a decade. In recent years it has established two incubators within Softopia Japan and VR Techno Japan. Unlike most of their once high-flying US and European counterparts, these incubators are non-profit, government-supported units, working in co-operation with academic institutions and private companies. Gifu's uniquely Japanese incubator model treats start-up companies not merely as moneymaking ventures as they are in the West, but as playing a vital role in the community. Overall, the Sweet Valley Project provides incubator facilities, research center venues, and training and development opportunities to support scientists, engineers, and entrepreneurs in the development of next-generation technologies and innovations.

Softopia Japan was created in 1996. In contrast to private science parks and incubators elsewhere in Japan and around the world, Softopia is completely non-profit. It provides state-of-the-art facilities to IT businesses (rent-free for up to three years) with the sole aim of promoting the region's IT industry and stimulating the local economy. It also conducts various joint research and development projects with academic and industrial partners domestically and world-wide. Its international software R&D center is a high-tech incubator complex designed by world-renowned architect Kisho Kurokawa. About 74 mainly high-tech companies are tenants of the facilities that include technology development labs. Softopia also provides training facilities and technical training to nurture talent in the IT field.

Softopia seeks to play a leading role in making Gifu Prefecture an international base for advanced information technology. To that end, Softopia recently completed an International Incubator Center to help foster development of information and communications technology industries. At this center, "start-ups and individual entrepreneurs receive considerable support in bringing their business ideas to life. Close to a dozen overseas companies have already begun operations in Sweet Valley."[9] To encourage a greater foreign business presence, Softopia offers a non-Japanese residential subsidy program through which non-Japanese employees of Softopia tenant companies may receive residential financial assistance of up to 27,000 yen in subsidies.

VR Techno Japan was launched in 1993 as a public/private partnership involving prefectural organizations and 40 private companies. It supports research on virtual reality technology, the development of new VR simulations, and the promotion of information exchange, all focused primarily on future manufacturing interests. Related industries include electronics, transportation, construction, and machinery. VR Techno Japan intends to become an international VR technology incubator center.

The VR Techno Center is a central facility that houses the Gifu Prefecture Science Technology Promotion Center, Gifu Prefecture's Technology Development Foundation, Gifu Prefecture Enterprise Secretariat, Gifu Prefecture Manufacturing Association, Gifu Technology Association, Kagamigahara City Office, Corporate Upgrade Support Center, similar public support organizations, and companies including the Gifu Prefecture Intellectual Property Center and a branch of the Invention Organization. Other companies have located around the main facility. The Annex Techno 2 facility is the venture support facility, much like Softopia's Dream Core that houses its International Incubation Center.

The Japanese are renowned for their investment in long-term planning. Given the vital importance of new technology, their non-profit incubator model may turn out to be an exceedingly wise long-term investment.

BUSINESS MODELS: MAGIC BULLET?

The e-dimension is clearly having a profound impact on business/organizational models. Countless experiments in new forms of organizing will come and go along the way. Consulting empires will be built – and broken – upon their ability to package and run with dynamic new models. There is even the potential for developing proprietary models. For example, the US patent and trademark office granted applications for patents to two e-businesses in 1998 (priceline.com and CyberGold Inc.) for their *business models*.[10] While it remains to be seen whether the courts will give their blessing, the patents suggest the potential power of an innovative model.

Nevertheless, Harvard professor Jeffrey Rayport notes, "there is an irony intrinsic to the mad rush to 'discover' the dominant Internet business model. What awaits us is the perhaps deflating realization that, Internet company valuations aside, e-commerce is just, when all is said and done, another kind of business. As with businesses that have come before it, there are countless "right" answers, endless combinations of business models and infinite permutations of key themes and approaches. There will be no magic bullet. No matter how often consultants and academics pretend that business is more science than art, every practitioner knows that business is almost all art, just as the genius of nearly every corporate strategy lies in its implementation."[11]

B-webs *sound* incredibly promising, but technological solutions do not guarantee effective implementation,[12] as any seasoned manager may attest. Thomas Davenport, professor of IS at Boston University School of Management and director of the Andersen Consulting Institute for Strategic Change, argues, "Sure, a lot of companies are forming networks. But isn't forming them easier than actually making them work? ... The sceptic in me feels that perhaps the greatest beneficiaries from all this network activity will be the lawyers ... It's pretty clear that success in many of these networks will require integration of processes across companies. Another phrase for this is 'inter-organizational re-engineering.' Still another phrase for this is 'too hard.' Remember how many companies failed at the 'intra-organizational' form of re-engineering? Think it gets any easier when the people who have to change their behavior don't even work for your company?"[13]

Ah yes, human behavior. Even a b-web enthusiast like Don Tapscott acknowledges that "technology alone is not making this happen; it also takes a culture skilled at establishing trust and sharing knowledge."[6] Similarly, Jeffrey Rayport suggests that "there are no simple answers. Every e-commerce business is either viable or not viable. They hardly qualify for the paint-by-number prescriptions that business people seem to expect. Business models themselves do not offer solutions; rather, how each business is run determines its success. So the success of e-commerce businesses will hinge largely on the art of management even as it is enabled by the science of technology. The scarce resource will be, as it is in practically all of business, the building block of free enterprise: entrepreneurial, and increasingly managerial, talent."[11]

KEY LEARNING POINTS

» Major shift from bureaucracy to "infocracy" in last 50 years.
» Shift from organizational models to business models.
» Two primary categories of e-business models:
   » those built "on the Internet"; and
   » those that develop and provide network infrastructure.
» Within each category there are three generic models:
   » producers;
   » distributors; and
   » portals.
» Business webs integrate many of the trends in organizational models. They are enabled by the Internet and new technologies.
» Business webs accelerate the dismantling of vertically-integrated organizational structures.
» Incubators are investment vehicles for launching high-tech start-ups. Some have declared the incubator age now dead.
» Japan is developing a non-profit public/private partnership international incubator model.
» Some business models may be patented in the US.
» There are no "magic bullet" models. E-business is just another business.

NOTES

1 Clawson, J. (2000) "The new infocracies: implications for leadership". *Ivey Business Journal*, May/June [London].

2 Rappa, M. "Business models on the Web." *Managing the Digital Enterprise*, an online course available at http://digitalenterprise.org/models/models.html

3 Chesbrough, H. & Rosenbroom, R.S. (2001) *"The role of the business model in capturing value from innovation: evidence from*

Xerox Corporation's technology spin-off companies." Paper to be submitted to Industrial and Corporate Change, available online at digitalenterprise.org/models/models.html

4 Applegate, L.M. (2001) "Building information age businesses for the twenty-first century." *E-Business Handbook* (ed. Lowry, P.B., Cherrington, J.O., & Watson, R.J.), CRC Press.

5 Tapscott, D., Ticoll, D., & Lowy, A. (2000) *Digital Capital: Harnessing the Power of Business Webs.* Harvard Business School Press, Boston, MA.

6 Robinson, B.D. (2000) *Don Tapscott: an interview with the cyber visionary.* Text available online at www.stockhouse.com/interviews/jun00/061600com_tapscott.asp

7 Barrett, N. *Surviving the internet revolution.* Online article available at www.businessnewsnow.com/storydetail.asp?storyid = 2778

8 Christopher, A. (2001) "Incubators lose favor, some still see potential." *Venture Capital Journal*, Wellesley Hills.

9 Anon. (2001) "An IT model for local development," *Focus Japan*, June [Tokyo].

10 Buchanan, L. (1998) "A business model of one's own." *Inc.*, November, Boston, MA.

11 Rayport, J.F. "The truth about internet business models: in the end, an e-business is just another business." Online article available at www.strategy-business.com/briefs/99301

12 See, for example, Fitzgerald, S.P. (2002) *Making Business Decisions in the Twenty-first Century.* Capstone Publishing, UK.

13 Davenport, T.H. (2000) "Nets upon nets." *CIO Magazine*, April Available online at www.cio.com/archive/040100/davenport.html

The Global Dimension of Organizational Models

This chapter addresses the impact of globalization on organizational models. Traditional approaches to globalization are embodied in four models: global, international, multinational/multidomestic, and transnational. The rapid development of network communication technologies gives rise to a fifth possibility: the virtual transnational. ASEA Brown Boveri is in the process of transforming itself into a virtual transnational. Finally, the impact of national cultures on organizational models is explored.

- » Organizational models for globalization:
  - » best practice: ASEA Brown Boveri.
- » The impact of culture:
  - » merging models across cultures – theories X, J and Z;
  - » cultural clusters of organizational models.
- » Key learning points.

The globalization of business is hardly new. The world's largest corporations have been establishing international operations through the greater part of the last century. The pace and scope of globalization, however, have accelerated tremendously in the past two decades. Now globalization is having a profound impact on all aspects of business and all types of companies, from global corporations to service providers in professional bureaucracies to "local" manufacturers. That impact is interwoven with that of the e-dimension to create powerful opportunities and threats simultaneously. In fact, the global and e-dimensions are so inextricably interlinked that it can be difficult to separate one from the other. "In the Internet era, local and international markets will become indistinguishable as this technology gives small companies a global reach and enables large ones to micro-tailor their businesses to individual consumers in virtually every neighborhood in the world"[1] notes Robert Hormats, vice chairman of Goldman Sachs International.

As the business world races toward a global future, the challenges are daunting. The Internet facilitates global reach, interaction, transaction, and collaboration, but does not diminish the complex web of socio-cultural, political, economic, and logistical factors that must be addressed in global organizations. "Globalization will not be smooth," Hormats warns. "As companies increase their investment abroad, rely more on overseas supplies, expand their international customer base, or broaden their range of foreign partnerships, the complexity of management challenges will grow exponentially. Several countries are taking steps to bring corporate law, accounting practices, and financial disclosure in line with international practices. However, legal and political systems, cultures, individual tastes, business practices, product safety requirements, and environmental standards will continue to differ among countries and often be sharply altered for years to come, demanding countless and rapid adjustments by international businesses."[1]

ORGANIZATIONAL MODELS FOR GLOBALIZATION

The forms that companies use to globalize have evolved – and continue to evolve – over time. In 1987 Christopher Bartlett and Sumantra Goshal distinguished four basic models in use: global, multinational, international, and transnational.[2] Each is designed to address one or more critical strategic issues, and differs from the others on various structural dimensions.

Global model

A global firm's headquarters is based in its home country, while its operations are located in several favorable foreign locations. Global firms are designed to maximize efficiency and profitability by taking advantage of economies of scale. Therefore, they tend to market standardized products and to minimize costly customization.

Global firms tend to be structured according to world-wide product divisions with some centralization of operating decisions, many co-ordinating mechanisms, and a high co-ordination need.[3] "Many domestic organizations adopted this approach in order to broaden their markets by exporting their product ... Many Japanese firms, such as Honda and Nissan, have used this approach to expand their markets within the United States."[4]

International model

An international firm typically locates separate manufacturing and marketing functions in each of its major market countries. However, it centralizes its research and development efforts in its home country. There is some limited customization for local markets.

These firms are structurally characterized by few co-ordinating mechanisms among international manufacturing and marketing operations, and decentralization of all operational decisions except those related to the firm's core competencies.[3] "An international strategy makes sense if a firm has a valuable core competency that indigenous competitors in foreign markets lack, and if the firm faces relatively weak pressures for local responsiveness and cost reductions."[3] Given the focus on transferring core competencies to foreign markets, the primary strategic focus in international firms is learning. US firms that expanded overseas in the 1950s and 1960s primarily adopted an international model. Examples include Proctor & Gamble, IBM, and McDonald's.

Multinational/multidomestic model

Multinational organizations are similar to internationals in that they too seek to transfer products and skills from home base to foreign markets. They also establish manufacturing and marketing functions in each market. However, unlike internationals, multinationals are characterized by the need to be highly responsive to local market conditions. This leads to extensive local customization of products, services, and marketing, and to locating separate R&D functions in each market as well.

Multinational/multidomestic firms may develop into "decentralized federations in which each national subsidiary functions in a largely autonomous manner. As a result, after a time they begin to lack the ability to transfer the skills and products derived from core competencies to their various national subsidiaries around the world."[3] Thus the multinational structure is differentiated by few if any integrating mechanisms among subsidiaries and the decentralization of operating decisions. Because each subsidiary is relatively autonomous and adapts to its local market environment, there is little need for a strong organizational culture that permeates the entire multinational structure.

Transnational model

The challenges associated with globalization are complex, as discussed above, regardless of the organizational model employed. However, the transnational strategy is the most complex because it seeks to maximize efficiency, responsiveness, and learning – in other words, it incorporates the primary goal of each of the three prior models. Bartlett and Goshal[2] advocate the adoption of the transnational model as essential to survival in the hyper-competitive global marketplace.

The transnational model challenges a major assumption that underlies the other three: that the home country is the only source of core competencies. Thus the most innovative, most effective products, services, skills, and processes may emerge from any part of the transnational, and ideally should flow to and among all of the other parts. Bartlett and Goshal call this "global learning."[2]

Transnationals are typically structured as informal matrices in which operational decisions are both centralized and decentralized. There is a very high need for co-ordination, integrating mechanisms, and a strong organizational culture that transcends borders.

Transnationals are also characterized by "geocentric" approaches to staffing.[3] Geocentric staffing is based on selection of the best candidates for key positions throughout the organization, regardless of their national origin. Global organizations also tend to use this approach, whereas multinationals employ a polycentric approach. In polycentric staffing, local nationals are hired to manage subsidiaries, but they are not considered for positions at corporate headquarters. Finally, internationals utilize an ethnocentric approach in which only those from the firm's home base are considered for management positions; local nationals are not hired for key management positions.

Firms that pursue aspects of a transnational strategy include Verifone, Inc. (a Hewlett Packard subsidiary), Unilever, and Caterpillar Tractor. The model is exceedingly difficult to implement, however. "The organizational problems associated with pursuing what are essentially conflicting objectives constitute a major impediment to the pursuit of a transnational strategy. Firms that attempt to pursue a transnational strategy can become bogged down in an organizational morass that only leads to inefficiencies. While no one doubts that in some industries the firm that can adopt a transnational strategy will have a competitive advantage, in other industries global, multidomestic, and international strategies remain viable."[3]

Virtual transnational model

The rapid evolution and integration of advanced communication technologies facilitates and powerfully enables globalization processes regardless of the particular organizational model employed. However, Marie-Claude Boudreau, Karen Loch, Daniel Robey, and Detmar Straud suggest "for many firms, the answer to the problem of going global is to adopt a virtual organizational design."[4] There are a variety of perspectives on what constitutes a "virtual organization" (see Chapter 8), but these authors provide three characteristics that help to define what they mean.

First, a virtual organization is based on a federation (or web) of collaborative relationships (see Chapters 4 and 6) with other organizations. "Although traditional organizations may also use partnerships and alliances, virtual organizations use the federation concept as their primary principle of organizing."[4] Nike, Reebok, and Sun Microsystems are examples of such virtual, federated systems.

Second, virtual organizations are able to function, to a large extent, relatively independent of geographic space and time. This ability is vital to transnational organizations with their very high need for co-ordination and integrating mechanisms that transcend global boundaries. It also supports their ability to be locally responsive while at the same time maintaining centralized co-ordination.

Finally, virtual organizations are extremely flexible and even amorphous. They are able to change shape rapidly in order to take advantage of fleeting market opportunities. (B-webs are clearly a technologically-enabled form of virtual organization.) "In more conventionally organized competitors, reaction time is slowed by rigid organizational structures. The most competitive companies have the dexterity to shift resources to capitalize on new opportunities, while less nimble competitors may be stuck with under-utilized resources."[4]

Information technology addresses a key challenge in the transnational model: co-ordination. Boudreau and colleagues describe the contribution that particular technologies can make to support the needs of transnationals. The article was written, however, before the advent of the sorts of "plug-and-play" business web enabling technologies described in Chapters 4 and 7. Thus it is likely that the *virtual* transnational form will become increasingly viable and prominent as barriers to its effective implementation are lessened over time.

ASEA BROWN BOVERI

Asea Brown Boveri (ABB, see www.ABB.com) is one of the most celebrated and reported-on – and until recently, complexly-structured – transnational companies of our time. ABB is routinely decorated with corporate baubles as Europe's most-admired company. With its headquarters in Zurich, Switzerland, ABB is now the world's leading power and automation technology company, employing 160,000 personnel in more than 100 countries.

A brief history

ABB came about from the merger of the Swedish company Asea, then led by the redoubtable Percy Barnevik, and the Swiss company Brown Boveri. It was the biggest cross-border merger since Royal Dutch Shell's oily coupling. Barnevik became the CEO of the resulting ABB and revolutionized its organization and performance until being succeeded by Lindahl in 1997.

Barnevik was famous for his 30% rule – whenever he took over a company, 30% of its headquarters staff were fired; 30% were moved to other companies in the group; and 30% were spun off into separate profit centers; leaving 10% to get on with the work – a radical "hollowing out" process akin to the shamrock organizational model (see Chapter 8).

Once the merger was announced on August 10, 1987, quite simply, Barnevik made it work. "The challenge set by Barnevik was to create – out of a group of 1300 companies employing 210,000 people in 150 countries – a streamlined, entrepreneurial organization with as few management layers as possible," wrote Kevin Barham and Claudia Heimer in their book *ABB – The Dancing Giant*.[5] To enable this to happen, Barnevik introduced a complex matrix structure – what Lindahl has called "decentralization under central conditions." The company, run by an executive committee, had been divided into some 35 business areas and 5000 profit centers, in addition to country organizations. The aim was to reap the advantages of being a large organization while also retaining the advantages of smallness.

ABB's matrix structure had been the source of much debate. It was complex, paradoxical, and ambiguous. However, it proved to be highly effective as a sophisticated means of managing this particular transnational. ABB's deep-rooted local presence, global vision, cross-border understanding, and global values, and its principles for managing creative tension, global connection at the top, and global ethics were key to making its highly complex model work. They reflect the very high need in transnational organizations for a strong organizational culture and integrating mechanisms that transcend global boundaries (see the section on transnational models, above). Last but certainly not least, CEO Barnevik's rare dynamism and intelligence were essential to making it work. Imitators beware!

Transforming the ABB model

In January 2001, under the leadership of president and CEO Jörgen Centerman, ABB began transforming its matrix into a "customer-centric" model (i.e. extremely responsive to highly localized needs). It is the first organization in its industry to align its structure with its customers and channels to market. The new model will result in four customer-based divisions – utilities; process industries; manufacturing and consumer industries; and oil, gas and petrochemicals – which are all supported by two generic product divisions – power technology and automation technology. The latter two divisions serve external channel partners, wholesalers, distributors, system integrators, and original equipment manufacturers. The seventh and final division, financial, remains unchanged and continues to serve all internal and external customers.

At the core of this global overhaul is the development and implementation of a common industrial IT architecture that will integrate all ABB products globally. This vividly illustrates the case made by Boudreau and colleagues back in 1998 for the role of IT in empowering the possibility of the virtual transnational organization. ABB's new integrative IT architecture will significantly increase its ability to meet all three strategic challenges of a transnational (responsiveness, efficiency, and learning), simultaneously while providing a common interface for all users to interact through. Finally, it is creating an internal incubator called New Ventures to nurture the development of new technologies.

THE IMPACT OF CULTURE

Culture influences models of organization in several ways. First, organizational models are culture-bound. Second, each culture contributes unique models and approaches to organizing that may enrich the

repertoire of models available. Finally, attempts to overlay a cultur-
ally inappropriate model may cause significant conflict and undermine
globalization efforts.

Merging models across cultures – theories X, J and Z

In some cases, diverse cultural models of organization may be integrated
to support more effective implementation across cultures. For example,
in 1978 Ouchi and Jaeger[6] contrasted the typical American bureaucracy
(Theory X) with the prevailing Japanese model of the day, which they
dubbed Theory J. Theory J organizations are primarily distinguished
by their emphases on lifetime vs. short-term employment, consensual
vs. individual decision-making, shared vs. individual responsibility for
outcomes, horizontal vs. vertical promotion, and holistic concern for
workers, among other characteristics. But some factors of the Japanese
model do not mesh well with American culture, and so it was modified
to fit American organizations more comfortably.

Ouchi and Jaeger called the resulting hybrid model Theory Z, which
combined the best features of both the American and Japanese models.
Characteristics of Theory Z organizations include a commitment to long-
term – though not necessarily lifetime – employment, holistic concern
for workers, and participative, consensual decision-making, but with
individual vs. collective responsibility given the American system.

Theory Z organizations are also more diverse than those of Theory
J, which tend toward ethnocentrism. Hiring practices in Theory J
organizations typically weed out those who would not blend into
the organization's culture – including women and minorities. While
this has also been the case in American organizations, the legal and
social climate has been changing since the Civil Rights Movement, and
to a certain extent large American bureaucracies have implemented
affirmative action programs to help recruit women and minorities
into these organizations. This emphasis on the heterogeneity of the
workforce is included in the Theory Z cultural hybrid model.

Ouchi subsequently published a best-selling book[7] on his Theory Z,
which created a lot of interest in organizational culture. He ascribed
the Z model to a handful of major American corporations, including
IBM, Intel, HP, Eli Lilly, and Eastman Kodak, primarily based upon their
participative, consensual approach to decision-making. However, he

observed that the model has downsides, which include a potential for fostering excessively clannish insularity and homogeneity, which can inhibit openness toward new ideas.

Cultural clusters of organizational models

Geert Hofstede, world-renowned expert on various differences among national cultures related to organizations and management, surveyed 100,000 employees of multinationals in more than 50 countries between 1967 and 1978 about their work-related values and organizational perceptions. He derived four value dimensions from these data:[8]

» **power distance** refers to the acceptable range of inequality in power between supervisors and subordinates;
» **uncertainty avoidance** indicates the level of acceptance or avoidance of risk and ambiguity;
» **individualism–collectivism** describes the degree to which the social framework is loosely (individualism) or tightly (collectivism) structured; and
» **masculinity–femininity** refers to gender-role patterns learned in each culture.

Hofstede later applied two of the dimensions – power distance and uncertainty avoidance – to map the differences among national cultures in their implicit preferences for organizational models. The results suggested four generic cultural models.[9]

» **Market model.** This is decentralized and informal, and is based on small power distance and weak uncertainty avoidance. Nations that prefer the market model include the US, Canada, Australia, the UK, Netherlands, and many Nordic countries.
» **Family model.** This is centralized and informal, and is based on large power distance with weak uncertainty avoidance. Several East Asian countries fit this profile, including Singapore, the Philippines, Hong Kong, and India.
» **Machine model.** This is formal but decentralized, and involves small power distance and strong uncertainty avoidance. National

cultures exhibiting this preference include Israel, Austria, Germany, Switzerland, and Finland.

» **Pyramid model.** This is both formal and centralized, and is based on large power distance and high uncertainty avoidance. A wide range of countries use this model, including France, Iran, Pakistan, Spain and most South American countries, some East Asian countries like Japan, Taiwan, and Thailand, and other Mediterranean nations like Italy, Greece, and the former Yugoslavia.

Of course these are sweepingly broad generalizations, and any generalizations about particular nations or cultures mask the profound diversity that exists within each culture. Still, there are significant differences among world cultures, and the diversity of cultural models increases the complexity of globalization.

Finally, **alliances** and **networks** are primary interorganizational models that firms use to support their globalization efforts. These collaborative forms range from highly-structured equity joint ventures to transitory virtual organizations. They are explored in the section on organizational collaboration in Chapter 6.

KEY LEARNING POINTS

» Globalization is having a profound impact on organizational models and all organizations.
» Globalization is extremely complex and will not be smooth.
» There are four basic organizational models for globalization, each with a different focus:
  » global - efficiency;
  » multinational - responsiveness;
  » international - learning; and
  » transnational - efficiency, responsiveness, and learning.
» The transnational model is most complex.
» IT increases the viability of the virtual transnational model.
» Cultural differences influence organizational models in several ways.
» Four generic models are implicitly preferred by different national cultures:

- » market model;
- » family model;
- » machine model; and
- » pyramid model.
- » The interplay of cultures can enrich organizational models. It can also lead to conflict and undermine globalization efforts.

NOTES

1 Hormats, R.D. (1999) "High velocity." *Harvard International Review,* Cambridge, MA.
2 Bartlett, C.A. & Goshal, S. (1987) "Managing across borders: new strategic requirements." *Sloan Management Review.*
3 Hill, C.W.L. (1997) *International Business,* 2nd edn. Irwin, Chicago.
4 Boudreau, M-C., Loch, K.D., Robey, D., & Straud, D. (1998) "Going global: using information technology to advance the competitiveness of the virtual transnational organization." *Academy of Management Executive.*
5 Barham, K. & Heimer, C. (1999) *ABB–The Dancing Giant: Creating the Globally Connected Corporation*, FT/Prentice Hall, London.
6 Ouchi, W.G. & Jaeger, A.M. (1978) "Type Z organizations: stability in the midst of mobility." *Academy of Management Review*, April.
7 Ouchi, W.G. (1981) *Theory Z: How American Business can Meet the Japanese Challenge.* Addison-Wesley Publishing, Reading, MA.
8 Hofstede, G. (1983) "The cultural relativity of organizational practices and theories." *Journal of International Business Studies*, Fall issue [London].
9 Hofstede, G. (1983) "National cultures in four dimensions: a research-based theory of cultural differences among nations." *International Studies of Management and Organization*, Spring/Summer issue [NY].

The State of the Art of Organizational Models

The state of the art in human organizing is complex and multi-faceted. This chapter begins with an examination of the model that everyone loves to hate – bureaucracy – and its relevance, if any, to today's models. Next, the rapid escalation of transorganizational collaboration is explored, along with structural models for collaboration. Finally, the implications of "chaordic" organizational models – the most radical yet natural of approaches to human organizing - are discussed.

» Bureaucracy: dead, dying, or immortal?
» Organizational collaboration:
    » structures of organizational collaboration;
    » vision and values: alternatives to hierarchy;
    » the future of organizational collaboration.
» Chaordic alliances:
    » business implications;
    » beyond business models: the big picture.
» Key learning points.

Just what is the "state of the art" in human organizing? What models hold the most promise? What are the most significant trends? Certainly the perpetuation of bureaucracy is not among them . . . is it?

In this chapter we shall deepen our exploration of these questions, which are addressed throughout this book. We'll begin with a post mortem on the widely assumed "death" of bureaucracy. That death has been trumpeted for more than 35 years now. So the burning question is, is bureaucracy dead yet? If not, just how close to the grave is it? And what role, if any, will bureaucracy play in organizational models of the twenty-first century?

The state of the art of modeling organizations is increasingly trans-organizational. As mentioned briefly in Chapter 5, alliances, networks, and other collaborative forms are primary vehicles for globalization, as well as for other strategic objectives like innovation and learning. The boundaries among firms are becoming increasingly blurred and less relevant as amorphous clusters of organizations, and interdependent constellations of those clusters, increasingly dominate the organizational landscape. These collaborative networks challenge our traditional models and conceptions of organization.

These collaborative forms, like those of individual organizations, range from highly formalized and centralized to very informal and decentralized. The most radical of these forms, the "chaordic alliance," teeters on the boundary between *chaos* and *order* (as does all of life in the universe as we now know it). Chaordic alliances epitomize the trends in organizational models over the past several decades. They also provide a compass toward a future of human organizing that is commensurate with the enormity of the challenges facing our globe, as well as with the infinite capacity of the human spirit to meet those challenges. This is the state of the art of organizational models in the twenty-first century.

BUREAUCRACY: DEAD, DYING, OR IMMORTAL?

In 1966, management visionary Warren Bennis heralded the death of bureaucracy. He "predicted that the ponderous decision-making and functional divisions of industrial age bureaucracy would render them obsolete."[1] Bennis based his views on four perceived threats to the bureaucratic form:[2]

» its inflexibility and inability to adapt to increasingly turbulent business environments;

» as an organization increases in size, inefficient and non-productive bureaucratic structures actually work to hamper growth;

» bureaucracy's rigid, hierarchical, and impersonal authority structures are not well suited to an increasingly diverse and highly specialized workforce; and

» managerial values and behaviors are changing away from mechanistic, coercive approaches associated with machine bureaucracies (this is McGregor's Theory X – see Chapter 3), toward more democratic and humanistic approaches to management (Theory Y) which, Bennis argued, were counter to the bureaucratic ideal.

In the decades since Bennis's proclamation, management thinkers have, by and large, buried the bureaucracy as a viable model, paid their respects, and moved on to invent a more scintillating kaleidoscope of organizational forms – some of which are discussed in this book. Yet take a quick tour of the current organizational landscape, and underneath the slimmed down, re-engineered, technology-driven, information-based organization, underneath the hoopla of legions of management gurus, you may be shocked to discover that the bureaucratic heart and soul is quite far from death and decay, or even from dying a long, slow, and painful death. In fact, you may discover that the newly svelte bureaucratic soul is quite vitally alive and healthy. Then again, that may not shock you, based upon your own personal experiences and on those of countless others; experiences which are informally expressed through the *Dilbert* cartoon series and others.

In fact as far back as 1970, Robert Miewald argued that the purported death of bureaucracy was greatly exaggerated, and that, contrary to popular belief, the bureaucratic model is in fact quite adaptable.[3] Certainly elements of the form have survived for several millennia (see Chapter 3, section *A bit of ancient history*). Miewald placed Weber's articulation of bureaucracy within the context of nineteenth-century technology (i.e. industrialization) and history (e.g. German authoritarianism). Within that context, Weber's model made sense. "He would hardly be surprised, however, to learn that more sophisticated means of controlling behavior have been invented. All he wanted was a scientifically-derived concept of efficiency and he certainly would not be aghast to find that his model had been modified to reflect new ways in which to improve on efficiency."[2]

The emergence of the professional model of bureaucracy (see Chapter 3) provides some evidence of the malleability of the bureaucratic form. Highly trained, skilled, and paid professionals constitute the operating core of professional bureaucracies. For these professionals, self-discipline is socialized via professional indoctrination, licensing regulations and so on, as opposed to being imposed primarily through bureaucratic rules within the organization (top-down rules and regulations, however, are still strongly imposed within the larger, parallel structures for administrative, non-professional support staff – see Chapter 3). As Robbin observes, "one can argue, in fact, that the professional bureaucracy has merely substituted the arrogance of high training [for] the arrogance of high office."[2]

More recently, in a 1992–93 survey[4], a significant majority of 500 managers of small to large companies world-wide said that their organizations continued to be hierarchically structured (see Chapter 3), although many were in the process of significant downsizing, restructuring, and/or re-engineering efforts (see the glossary in Chapter 8). What makes the bureaucratic form so resilient, in spite of massive efforts to transform traditional structures? In 1990, Stephen Robbins suggested seven possible causes.[2]

1 Bureaucracy simply works, and it has worked regardless of technologies and environments, over time.
2 Size rules. Successful organizations tend to get bigger, bureaucracies work most effectively in large organizations, and size may even determine structure, thereby *causing* bureaucracy.
3 Features of bureaucracy are "naturally selected" for survival from among competing organizational models because they are more effective at promoting efficiency.
4 Managers and workers alike continue to value order, regularity, rationality, goal orientation, and standardization of goods, services, and procedures. In America, freedom is understood to entail adherence to rules and regulations, and subordination to authorities (e.g. the police, the courts).

5 Environments are not really as turbulent as they are purported to be, and managerial action helps reduce the impact of environmental uncertainties.
6 The bureaucratic model has already exhibited successful adaptation to the demands of the knowledge age in the form of the professional bureaucracy.
7 Those in power in organizations choose models – and technologies – that perpetuate their ability to maintain control. Bureaucracy enables them to do that exceedingly well.

This combination of factors led Robbins to conclude that the bureaucratic form may be immortal (a similar argument, however, could probably be made for the enduring and globally ubiquitous family business model). But what about the Internet? What about dot-coms? What about e-business? The above research and arguments all pre-date the Internet revolution. Surely high-tech innovators are challenging the very foundations of bureaucracy, aren't they?

Perhaps. I posed those very questions to Stephen Robbins, a long-time observer of organizations and the author of numerous books on management, organizational behavior, organizational theory, human resource management, conflict resolution, and supervision. "Computerization has really revised the way we look at organizations," he says. "Most of the organizational structure elements that we talked about have become obsolete. I do think that the old model doesn't work anymore, and that it's a different ballgame. Networks have changed organizations, and my feeling is that managers can use these new tools to give the appearance of decentralization and the appearance of empowerment, when in fact they still have controls that allow them to monitor and intercede when they want to."[5]

Remember that high degrees of formalization and standardization are key aspects of bureaucracy. Think about the new infocracies, built around massive data, information, and knowledge management systems, customer relationship management, etc. These systems provide ready access to information and analytic tools and reports that are highly standardized, yet also customizable to a pre-specified degree.

The point is that information systems, analytic tools, and access to them have become – and perhaps need to be – highly formalized. In many organizations you need special training to learn how to use their customized, standardized software, communication, and networking systems. And management can still control who has access to what systems, tools, and information. They select technologies that enable them to do so. In an even broader, global context, think of Microsoft, attempting to impose its system on all users world-wide.

Information revolution aside, intranets and Internet may not necessarily toll the death bell of bureaucracy. As Robbins notes, "whether bureaucracy exists or not is one of definition. The idea of bureaucracy was basically standardization – and you can get it in more than one way, whether in the form of McDonald's, or in the way they do it in a Big-5 accounting firm, or in a group of software engineers."[5]

Thus the primary targets for standardization are shifting away from rigidly-defined jobs and procedures (in some cases) toward the currency of the new age: knowledge and information. Further, strong organizational missions, values, and cultures could also be viewed as alternative means toward the same ends of standardization and reducing uncertainty. "When you have a strong culture, you override the need for formalization, standardization, and documentation," Robbins notes. "When you carefully select, socialize, and indoctrinate employees into the organization, they buy into the system, so you have the same outcome with a different process. You see this particularly in professional organizations.

"Defining an organization's mission and values, its purpose and principles, could be seen as a different form of standardization," Robbins continues. "But you have to be careful to create a statement that is clear enough to give the outcomes that you want, yet at the same time provides enough flexibility so that people can make judgments within a range of possibilities.

"Standardization has to work with this seemingly conflicting need for flexibility. As environments change more quickly, developing a strong culture and mission statement becomes increasingly important. We need to have an overall idea that we know what we are trying to do, and that we have some discretion within a range as to how to do it, but at all times we will test it to see if our actions are consistent with our mission and values.

"Think of it as two conflicting goals that you are trying to balance. That is what the whole mechanistic/organic argument is about. Most organizations try to minimize the impact of change on them so that they can maintain a more mechanistic structure, rather than developing an adaptive, organic model that is flexible to change. Management will continue to *try* to maintain bureaucratic structures because of the efficiencies and controls they can provide. Can they always pull it off? No."[5]

Hierarchy is another integral feature of bureaucracy. Ron Ashkenas, one of the authors of *The Boundaryless Organization*,[6] champions breaking down vertical barriers in organizations. However, he says "the vertical hierarchy is an easy target for blame and criticism, but in fact some sort of vertical structure seems almost hardwired into human experience, beginning with the family. This form has persisted because it works. There will always be a need for leaders and followers. There can be no doubt, however, that an overly rigid system of top-down control drastically impedes organizational speed of response. When a firm is being crippled by vertical barriers, it will exhibit [dysfunctional] symptoms."[7]

Bureaucracies may be flatter, slimmer, and technologized, they may look amorphous, democratic, and even virtual, but bureaucracies and hierarchies are hardly dead. Perhaps killing and burying them is not the issue. After all, thousands of years worth of managerial wisdom can't be *all* wrong, can it? Perhaps the state of the art in organizational models includes learning from history and adapting the best of the bureaucratic model to the demands of the world of today.

ORGANIZATIONAL COLLABORATION

One of the most profound dynamics of the past two decades has been the extraordinary proliferation of collaboration among organizations. Back in 1965, Emery and Trist[8] first prophesied that such a trend would develop in response to increasingly turbulent and uncertain environments. That trend shows no signs of abating as the ground swell of technological change and globalization continues to intensify.

A dizzying array of collaborative interorganizational models has evolved along the way. Those models range from dyadic partnerships engaged in short-term local projects, to world-wide constellations of organizations and citizens networked together to generate global social change. For example, **inter-sectoral partnerships** link government, business, non-governmental organizations (NGOs), and communities in addressing areas of common concern. Businesses enter intranational and international **joint ventures**, **alliances**, **networks**, and other forms of business collaboration in order to reap the benefits of mutual learning, exploration, development, and economic advantage. B-webs are but the latest, technologically-enabled, expression of this decades-long trend.

Yet within a Western cultural context, co-operative ventures have traditionally "been viewed as options that are undertaken reluctantly, often under external mandates such as government investment laws or in order to cross protectionist entry barriers in regulated economies."[9] In fact, it seems that many organizational theorists still feel the need to justify collaboration as necessary in order to *compete* more effectively, as if collaboration were in some way deviant from otherwise healthy competitive behavior.

Times, however, are changing. For example, Rupert Chisolm provides a detailed comparison of the industrial and post-industrial worldviews: "First, the industrial (atomistic) view of the external world is based on the law of the jungle (looking out for oneself) and a belief in the 'invisible hand,' the self-regulating system of classical economics. In contrast, the post-industrial view stresses co-operation in social systems: individuals, groups, organizations, and nations must work together for the good of the whole. The new beliefs of the post-industrial era clearly emphasize increased interaction among growing numbers of groups, organizations, and societies. Interorganizational networks will provide a primary way of fostering new beliefs and putting them into practice."[10]

Thus collaboration has become *de rigueur*. Some business thinkers even go so far as to herald the death of competition.[11] Ironically, these beliefs may only be "new" within the framework of the culturally-embedded Western rational economic model.

Interorganizational collaboration is very complex, technologically-enabled b-webs notwithstanding. A plethora of differences and obstacles must be bridged. Multiple formal and informal organizational systems, structures, goals, objectives, competencies, and cultures (and people!) must work together effectively toward a common purpose. Historical animosities and deeply entrenched cultural and institutional barriers must be transcended and transformed. Opportunities, risks, and uncertainties abound. Yet these substantial challenges have not stopped or even slowed the collaborative gold rush.

Something as seemingly simple as identifying membership can in fact be rather complex in alliances and networks. Although it may be relatively straightforward in contractually-based entities like equity joint ventures, it may be less so in many other collaborative models. For example, "it is difficult to conceptualize individuals as members of alliances in the same way they are viewed as organization members. By their very character, many alliances do not contain individuals full time."[12] Some members' involvement in the alliance may be pervasive and ongoing, whereas other members' involvement may be marginal and/or sporadic. In some forms of alliances members' involvement levels may span a wide range.

STRUCTURES OF ORGANIZATIONAL COLLABORATION

The traditional elements of intra-organizational structure – formalization, centralization, and complexity (see Chapter 2) – have also been applied to the analysis of interorganizational structure.[13] For example, Whetten used formalization as one distinguishing characteristic in his typology of collaborative forms.[14] Centralization involves decision-making control and influence in the alliance, and complexity "refers to the number of differentiated elements that must be contended with and integrated in order for [an alliance] to act as a unit."[13]

In models of organizational collaboration, structure may also be thought of as a composite of formal and informal control mechanisms. Formal structural features include things like the relative levels of equity/ownership and decision-making control, and the extent of any structured integrating or monitoring mechanisms. Informal structural features include, but are certainly not limited to, members' levels of overall power and influence, behavioral norms, and roles. Although informal structure plays a vital role in all alliances, its influence surpasses that of formal structure in alliances that rank low on formalization.

Prior to the 1980s, the study of collaborative models centered on parent–subsidiary configurations within multinational corporations.

During the 1980s, however, researchers became increasingly aware of other forms of organization that fell between the ideal types of markets and hierarchies. Powell contrasted markets and hierarchies with networks.[15] He viewed market forms of organization as based upon contracts, prices, and their enforcement, and network forms as based upon relationships and reciprocity.

Markets and hierarchies now form the termini of what has become the most widely adopted typology of structural business models. Collaborative forms are arranged on a continuum between those termini, ranging from contracts and agreements (near markets) to equity relationships (near hierarchies). For example, Contractor and Lorange[16] differentiate collaborative business forms according to increasing interdependence, with technical training and production/assembly/buyback agreements at the low end (near open markets), non-equity co-operative agreements in the middle, and equity joint ventures at the high end (near hierarchies). Typically, collaboration becomes more challenging as the level of interdependence involved increases.

VISION AND VALUES: ALTERNATIVES TO HIERARCHY

Emery and Trist were perhaps the first to highlight the central importance of emergent, implicit "values that have overriding significance for all members of the field. Social values here are regarded as coping mechanisms that make it possible to deal with persisting areas of relevant uncertainty."[17] They saw values as an alternative to hierarchy in controlling complex, highly interdependent matrix organizations. Similarly, Ouchi argues that common values and beliefs are important modes of control within highly interdependent intra-organizational systems that he calls "clans."[18]

In fact, the development of shared vision, purpose and goals is at the heart of a variety of collaborative forms. "This vision provides the context that orients all network activity. Retaining this orientation is critical to developing and maintaining networks."[10] And some forms of alliances are "held together to an extreme degree by their centralizing vision rather than an authority structure . . . or economic goals."[19]

THE FUTURE OF ORGANIZATIONAL COLLABORATION

What, then, will the future of organizational/business models look like? Will there be bureaucracies? Most likely. Autocracies? For sure, at least among a swathe of young entrepreneurial start-ups. Matrices? Of course. B-webs? Transnationals? Yes! Yes! Yes! The answer is not *either/or*, it's *yes/and*, with a bewildering array of new models erupting on the scene at a dizzying pace.

And that pace will continue to accelerate in this information age. Business and social visionary Dee Hock[20] observes that "the greater the capacity to receive, store, utilize, transform, and transmit information, the more diverse and complex the entity."[21]

He also notes that "Suddenly, with the revolution in micro-electronic technology, in the past 20 short years we have on the order of one thousand times better algorithms, five hundred thousand times more computing power per individual, and five hundred million times more mobility of information. The entire collective memory of the species (all known and recorded information), will soon be no more than a few keystrokes away.

"Yet, that is nothing. Just around the corner are other revolutions of much greater significance, such as nano- and bio-technology. Within two decades, we will be constructing organs, organisms, products, and services from the atom up. The capacity to receive, utilize, store, transform, and transmit information thousands of times greater than we now experience will be at the heart of it. The message is simple:

"Fasten your seat belts, the turbulence has scarcely begun. Unless evolution has radically changed its ways, we are facing an explosion of societal diversity and complexity incomparably greater than we now experience, or yet comprehend. And, we're going to manage such an explosion of societal diversity and complexity with our old, mechanistic, seventeenth-century, command-and-control notions of organization? Not the chance of a snowball in that proverbial hot place! It demands more than developing, re-organizing and re-engineering organizations, it demands that we re-conceive them in the most fundamental sense."[22]

Dee Hock did exactly that in creating VISA. "In the beginning, no one thought such an organization could be brought into being. But, in June, 1970, we proved ourselves wrong and the VISA Chaord came into being: a non-stock, for-profit, organization with ownership in the form of irrevocable, non-transferable, rights of participation. It transcends language, currency, politics, economics, and culture to connect successfully a bewildering variety of more than 20,000 financial institutions, 20 million merchants, and a billion people in 220 countries and territories. Annual volume approaches $1.8trn, continuing to grow in excess of 20% compounded annually with no end in sight.

"As the organization skyrocketed past $100bn of volume, it was co-ordinated by less than 500 people, none were recruited from business schools, none could own shares or acquire wealth for their services. Yet those people, without consultants, selected the VISA name and completed the largest trademark conversion in commercial history in a third of the time anticipated. They created the prototype of the present communications systems in ninety days for less than $30,000. Those systems now clear more electronic transactions in a week than the entire US Federal Reserve System does in a year.

"I tell you these few things to make a single point that we have somehow lost sight of in our present organizations: the truth is, that given the right chaordic organizations, from no more than dreams, determination, and the liberty to try, quite ordinary people consistently do extraordinary things."[22]

CHAORDIC ALLIANCES

You may be wondering at this point what "chaord" means, and what precisely a "chaordic" organization or alliance is. Hock defines a chaord as "(*i*) any self-organizing, adaptive, non-linear, complex *organism, organization* or *system, whether physical, biological or social*, the behavior of which harmoniously blends characteristics of both chaos and order; (*ii*) an entity whose behavior exhibits observable patterns and probabilities not governed or explained by its constituent parts; and (*iii*) an entity characterized by the fundamental organizing principles of nature."[22]

Chaordic organizations are low – very low – on formalization and centralization. They exemplify the power of shared purpose and principles to unify highly complex organizations (see the section above, *Vision and values: alternatives to hierarchy*).

They self-organize and self-govern around these shared, co-created values in order to serve their common purpose through a proliferation of multiple, random organizing experiments throughout the network. Those experiments will generate successes that may be retained, and failures that will be discarded. Yet the common purpose and principles endure. Co-operation and competition co-exist within chaordic organizations.

The "Chaordic Commons" is itself a chaordic alliance whose purpose is to develop, disseminate, and implement new concepts of organization that result in more equitable sharing of power and wealth, improved health, and greater compatibility with the human spirit and biosphere. The Website (www.chaordic.org) provides information and resources on the nature of chaordic systems, with a library of materials that includes definitions, characteristics, an overview of the pilot projects in chaordic organizing, articles, speeches, a reading list, and more. The site also provides information and materials on becoming an owning member of the organization, and on activities and workshops on creating chaordic organizations.

Years after retiring from VISA, Hock was approached by the Joyce Foundation to discover what it would take to create the sort of massive, global institutional reinvention that VISA exemplified. Since then he has been working extensively with half a dozen vast experiments in the possibility of chaordic organization (see www.chaordic.org). For example, he "just finished working with the Federal GeoData Committee. That committee was formed by the US government to require all of the federal agencies involved in geodata to work together across their boundaries. That involves 81,000 institutions in the US, a good many of which are corporations. Police and fire departments, the forestry service, and many other kinds of organizations participate in this geophysical data industry for tracking information, etc. If we are ever going to have a cohesive network that can be used productively by both public and private sector organizations, it must be across all of the sectors."[22]

A particularly inspiring example (modelled on Hock's chaordic work) is the birth of the United Religions Initiative (URI), whose purpose is to "promote enduring, daily interfaith co-operation, to end religiously motivated violence, and to create cultures of peace, justice, and healing for the Earth and all living beings" (www.uri.org). People from diverse religions, spiritual expressions, and indigenous traditions came together from around the world over a five-year period to develop the purpose and principles that are at the heart of the URI. This level of interfaith co-operation is unprecedented in human history. Since the formal signing of the URI charter in 2000, over 150 "co-operation circles" – the base organizing unit of this chaordic alliance – have already formed on every continent around the world. Additional information on and examples of chaordic organizations are available at www.chaordic.org.

Our very notions of organization, sectors, models, and structures begin to dissolve in the chaordic age. Hock explains: "we are in an unprecedented moment in time when the capacity to receive, store, utilize, transform and transmit information has completely escaped the boundaries of all existing forms of organization – nation states, cities, corporations, universities, churches, families, communities, whatever. It is transcending and enfolding them into new, much more complex and diverse systems and entities, the shape of which is only dimly perceived. Today, we don't know where a business begins or ends – what the distinction is between supplier, manufacturer, distributor, retailer, consumer, and banker, or if those concepts are even useful in thinking about it. We don't know what the functional boundaries of a nation state really are. The distinctions between races, cultures and beliefs are increasingly blurred. Old concepts of organization are dissolving before our eyes and we grow desperate trying to make new, societal realities conform to old notions of organization. In all of recorded history that has never worked, and it won't work this time either."[22]

Business implications

But what does this mean for your business? Should you eradicate centralized command-and-control structures as quickly as you can? Not necessarily. "There's always some sense of hierarchy and some sense of command and control," Hock says. "Your body fluctuates within certain limits or you die. A few months ago I went for cataract surgery. The last thing I wanted was a chaordic operating room. Command and control has its place and its uses. Nature uses it to some extent as well. Mother bears are known to swat their cubs. You could call that command and control, or maybe it's just a warning device until the cubs' own warning devices have matured. Fundamentally it's a whole new way of consciousness, but things have always functioned this way.

"Commercial organizations would be insane to destroy their current systems. That's the old destruction and reconstruction model. Don't destroy one and replace it with another; that's madness. You're assuming that *chaordic* is a noun, a thing. It is really an adjective that describes characteristics of organizing. "Chaordic" refers to the way the universe organizes. It's the oldest way of thinking; it's nothing new and radical. What's new and radical is Newton and Descartes postulating 400 years ago that the universe and all it contains could only be understood as machine-like structures with separable parts acting on one another with precise, linear laws of cause and effect.

"If you look at outsourcing, that's a manifestation of what I'm talking about. All of the alliances, that's what I'm talking about. The need for alliances and outsourcing is clearly a manifestation of chaordic principles in the commercial world. Business organizations that have characteristics of chaordic organizing include Royal Dutch Shell, which has traditionally organized its consortium this way, Semler Industries in Brazil, and Oticon, the Danish hearing aid company."[22]

BEYOND BUSINESS MODELS: THE BIG PICTURE

Beyond the highly conceptual and hyper-competitive world of business and organizational models lie the daunting global challenges that we face in the new millennium – challenges at the heart of human organizing. "The world faces a host of complex social, economic, ethnic, political, and security challenges," notes Robert Hormats, vice chairman of Goldman Sachs International. "Nuclear terrorism is a growing threat ... risking the sale of 'loose nukes' or deadly chemical and biological weapons that can be smuggled into cities anywhere in the world. The human, political, and economic implications of the use of such weapons would be catastrophic. Inequality between the richest and poorest societies creates a social tinderbox, made worse by the potential for growing ethnic strife, as demonstrated in Kosovo. Sustained high unemployment or financial disruptions could lead to a retreat from open markets or free-market capitalism in many countries.

"More than ever, business will have the opportunity to improve virtually every aspect of human life. But the emerging, high-tech, super-charged, global economy will not be the end of history, geography, or social strife. It will not eliminate the potential for human mistakes or irrational acts. [This] century opens full of promise, but whether it fulfils that promise will depend on what we make of it."[23]

But will business rise to meet that opportunity? For Dee Hock, the path is clear. "Next quarter's profit may be essential, but it's not a damned bit important to the universe, to nature, or to anybody's life. Devoting your life to next quarter's profit is nothing but to be a lackey to the world's wealthy and powerful, and they are willing to give you a dribble of it if you are willing to devote your life to greed and avarice. Look at the world with the eyes of the least privileged people on earth, and through the eyes of nature and the environment and what we're doing to it. Don't look at the stock market. Greed is driving it. There's nothing under it.

"In trillions of logical, rational, isolated acts, we pour billions of tons of 70,000 man-made toxic substances into the biosphere that it cannot recycle, punch holes in the ozone layer, pile up countless tons of virulent poisons with a half-life of 24,000 years, destroy at an accelerating rate the remaining 30% of our topsoil, pollute the remaining 50% of our fresh water, force 85% of the earth's people to exist on 15% of the resources, push two out of six people into abysmal poverty, and commit countless other disconnected acts with virtually no understanding that they are cumulative atrocities, or how they are combining to affect the planet, our lives, and the lives of our grandchildren.

"We don't have a welfare problem, an environmental problem, a crime problem, a climatic change problem, a population problem, or an economic problem. And we don't have an educational problem.

They are symptom not disease. At bottom, we have an *institutional* problem, and until we properly diagnose and deal with it, all societal problems will get progressively worse. There is simply no way to govern the diversity and complexity of twenty-first century society or our enormous capacity to interfere with biospheric and genetic systems with separatist, specialist, mechanistic, seventeenth-century concepts of organization.

"We are at that very point in time when a 400-year-old age is rattling in its death bed and another is struggling to be born: a shifting of culture, science, society, and institutions incomparably greater and swifter than the world has ever experienced. There isn't the slightest doubt in my mind that chaordic we are, chaordic we will remain, chaordic the world is, chaordic our institutions must become, and a chaordic leader every individual must be. It is the way of the world as life evolves into ever-increasing diversity and complexity.

"The only question is whether we will get there through massive institutional failure, enormous social carnage, regression into even more mechanistic pyramids of power and their inevitable collapse with even more carnage before new concepts can emerge. Or have we, at long, long last, evolved to the point of sufficient intelligence and will to create the conditions by which chaordic institutions can come into being? Institutions capable of their own continual learning and transformation; institutions which can harmoniously co-evolve with all other institutions, with all people and with all other living things to the highest potential of each and all.

"If not such new chaordic concepts of organization and leadership, then what? If not you, then who? If not now, then when? My deepest conviction is that you can discover such new concepts and live them to the full. My greatest hope is that you will. My sincerest wish is that all people may do so together."[22]

Conclusion

Organizations – and the conceptual models through which we envision them – are, quite literally, figments of our individual and collective imaginations. Thus the questions at the heart of the future of human organizing are "what are the highest hopes and possibilities that we can imagine?'' and ''how can we align our processes and models of organizing with those of natural systems so as no longer to harm ourselves, others, or life on Earth?'' Then, borne on the wings of imagination, and drawing upon the rich wisdom of people in all sectors and cultures, including the best of all of their models of organizing, we just might succeed in saving our precious planet for the generations that we hope are yet to come.

KEY LEARNING POINTS

The bureaucratic model is:

» far from dead, and perhaps immortal;
» at least somewhat adaptable; and is
» based on standardization, which can be achieved in multiple ways, including through knowledge and information systems, and/or organizational culture.

Organizational collaboration:

» has proliferated in the past two decades;
» is integral to the state of the art of organizational models;
» is very complex;
» becomes more challenging as the level of interdependence increases; and
» is made possible by shared vision, purpose, and goals.

Chaordic alliances:

» epitomize the most advanced trends in processes of organizing;
» are self-organizing and self-governing;
» balance competition and co-operation;
» transcend traditional notions of organization, sectors, models, and structures; and
» provide a compass toward a future of human organizing that is commensurate with the enormity of the challenges facing our globe, as well as with the infinite capacity of the human spirit to meet those challenges.

NOTES

1 Clawson, J. (2000) "The new infocracies: implications for leadership." *Ivey Business Journal*, May/June [London].

2 Robbins, S.P. (1990) *Organization Theory, Structure, Design, and Applications*, 3rd edn. Prentice Hall, Englewood Cliffs, NJ.

3 Miewald, R.D. (1970) "The greatly exaggerated death of bureaucracy." *CA Management Review*, Winter issue.

4 Applegate, L.M. (1993) *Business Transformation Self-assessment: Summary of Findings, 1992-93*. Case no. 194–013, Harvard Business School, Boston, MA.

5 Author interview.

6 Ashkenas, R.N., Ulrich, D., Prahalad, C.K., Jick, T., & Kerr, S. (1995) *The Boundaryless Organization: Breaking the Chains of Organizational Structure*. Jossey-Bass, San Francisco.

7 Ashkenas, R. (1999) "Creating the boundaryless organization (Innovations in business management). *Business Horizons*, September.

8 Emery, F. & Trist, E.L. (1965) "The causal texture of organizational environments." *Human Relations*.

9 Li, J. & Shenkar, O. (1998) "The perspectives of local partners: strategic objectives and structure preferences of international co-operative ventures in China," In Beamish, P.W. & Killing, J.P. (eds), *Co-operative strategies: Asian Pacific perspectives*. The New Lexington Press, San Francisco.

10 Chisolm, R. (1998) *Developing Network Organizations*. Addison-Wesley, Reading, Massachusetts.

11 Moore, J.F. (1996) *The Death of Competition: Leadership and Strategy in the Age of Business Ecosystems*. HarperBusiness, New York.

12 Osborn, R.N. & Hagedoorn, J. (1997) "The institutionalization and evolutionary dynamics of interorganizational alliances and networks." *Academy of Management Journal*.

13 Van de Ven, A.H. (1976) "On the nature, formation, and maintenance of relations among organizations," *Academy of Management Review*.

14 Whetten, D.A. (1987) "Interorganizational relations." In Lorsch J.W. (ed.) *Handbook of Organizational Behavior*. Prentice Hall, Englewood Cliffs, NJ.

15 Powell, W.W. (1990) "Neither market nor hierarchy: network forms of organization." In: Cummings, L.L. & Staw, B.M. (eds) *Research in Organizational Behavior*. JAI Press Inc.

16 Contractor, F.J. & Lorange, P. (1988) "Why should firms co-operate? The strategy and economics basis for co-operative ventures." In: Contractor, F.J. & Lorange, P. (eds) *Co-operative Strategies in International Business*. Lexington Books, Lexington, Massachusetts.

17 Emery, F. & Trist, E.L. (1965) "The causal texture of organizational environments." *Human Relations*.

18 Ouchi, W.G. (1980) "Markets, bureaucracies, and clans." *Administrative Science Quarterly*.

19 Waddock, S.A. & Post, J.E. (1995) "Catalytic alliances for social problem solving." *Human Relations*.

20 In 1991 Dee Hock was named one of the 30 living Laureates of the Business Hall of Fame. In 1992 he was recognized as one of eight people in the last quarter of the twentieth-century who most changed the way people live.

21 Hock, D.W. (1998) *An epidemic of institutional failure*. Keynote address, Organization Development Network annual conference, New Orleans, LA, November 16. Full text available online at www.ODNetwork.org/confgallery/deehock.html.

22 Author interview, September 26, 2001.

23 Hormats, R.D. (1999) "High velocity." *Harvard International Review*, Summer.

Organizational Model Success Stories

Three exemplary cases are presented that illustrate the state of the art in business and organizational models. First, the story of Bowstreet, Inc. highlights the transformation of an organization into a business web, and the rapid development of technology that enables that. Second, The Thread, Inc. illustrates the dramatic possibilities of the implementation of business webs in the apparel industry. Finally, worker democracies – exemplified by the Mondragon co-operatives, the world's most successful incubator of start-up enterprises – offer a vital alternative to the corporate shareholder model.

» Spinning b-webs with Bowstreet, Inc.:
  » Web services and business webs;
  » walking the b-web talk.
» The Thread weaves apparel industry b-webs:
  » the apparel industry: challenges and opportunities;
  » the solution;
  » roll out the b-webs – and let the savings begin!
» Incubating worker democracies: the Mondragon model:

» a tale of two Mondragons;
» principles of Mondragon's success;
» Mondragon is not alone.
» Key learning points.

Given the range, diversity, and rapid proliferation of models of business organizations, there are legions of success stories waiting to be told. Here are three exciting tales brought to you from the wild frontiers. The first clarifies the rather nebulous concept of web services. It illustrates the accelerating trend toward disaggregating organizational competencies, and shows how an organization can evolve itself into a business web over time. The second case sets all of this in motion in the story of a business that powerfully enables the rapid formation and dissolution of transitory virtual alliances in the apparel industry. The final story challenges the prevailing corporate shareholder model as being "the only way," or even the best way. It demonstrates that social vision and values expressed through worker democracy and ownership offer a viable, inspiring, and thriving alternative.

SPINNING B-WEBS WITH BOWSTREET, INC.

Business webs sound great in theory, but anyone who has been around the technology implementation block a few times can attest to the frequently agonizing challenges that must be overcome in integrating new information systems – whether into a company's existing internal systems or with those of its value-chain partners. But not any more! Bowstreet, Inc. is rapidly transforming companies' technological coupling abilities, enabling the rapid procreation of spontaneous strategic e-liances and collaborative e-business models. This newfound speed and ease has exponentially lowered the transaction costs associated with business partnering, thus eliminating both the economic and technical barriers to e-business collaboration.

Bowstreet (www.bowstreet.com), based in Portsmouth, New Hampshire, is a recognized leader in Web services; it automates the design and assembly of composite Web applications and promotes use and re-use of components across related families of applications, thereby enabling greater efficiency in successive development efforts. Bowstreet's automation technology dramatically reduces the cost and effort needed to create, update, and maintain families of Web applications used in a business web.

Bowstreet's pioneering Web services automation system, the Bowstreet™ Business Web Factory, brings massive economies of scale to e-business. Using that system, IT people can now create reusable application models that business people can then "mass-customize" and manage – *without programming or help from IT specialists* – for their customers, partners, and employees.

A privately-held company (with a stable full of heavy-hitting investors like Goldman Sachs, AOL, Morgan Stanley Dean Witter, Novell, and Oracle, among many others), Bowstreet was founded in January 1998 on the idea that companies will compete on the services they provide, not on the products they sell. Co-founders are former Tivoli chairman and CEO Frank Moss, and Preferred Systems co-founders Jack Serfass, David Sweet, and Joe Sommers. In August 1999, Bob Crowley (formerly of Arbortext and Kenan Systems) joined as president and CEO.

Bowstreet clients range from major corporations to innovative start-ups in a variety of sectors. They include, among others, Cisco Systems, CNA, Compaq, GE Small Business Solutions, John Crane, MetLife, Pitney Bowes Capital Services, SONICblue, and The Thread. Bowstreet has also assembled a top-flight list of technology partners to help it usher in the new age of b-webs. Partners include BEA Systems, Hewlett Packard, IBM, Interwoven, Netegrity, Novell, Oracle, Sun Microsystems, Vitria, and webMethods, among others. These partners supply solutions that complement Bowstreet's technology and that help customers achieve the highest performance and maximum flexibility in their b-web solutions.

Web services and business webs

Web services are being embraced by leading global companies and technology visionaries as the wave of the future, due to their ability to bypass technological roadblocks caused by proprietary IT systems. As platform-neutral, Internet-resident application components, Web services enable business partners to exchange services and information directly online. They are essentially digitized organizational competencies – service components that had previously been internalized within an organization – now dismantled, disaggregated, and digitized for consumption on the Web. They naturally extend and radically accelerate the trend toward the hollowing out of organizations through the outsourcing of non-core functions (see Chapter 8).

Steve Chazin, Bowstreet's director of product marketing, explains that "business webs are made possible by the ability to plug and play those Web services at will, and to customize the way they work together in a value chain or b-web. That's where we add our special sauce, what makes us unique. We build models that change the way the components behave. Companies digitize their assets in order to make what they do available over the Web. They package it in such a way that any company can come along and use their Web service, without having to do a lot of tight back-end integration development work to make that possible.''

Up until now, every time two companies wanted to do business together, add a new customer or supplier, their IT specialists had to do a development project for that particular partner. It was like agreeing to have the ends of two different water hoses use the same coupling, and then having to engineer that specific coupling. Now two companies can automatically plug their back-end systems into one another without that labor-intensive development work, thanks to Bowstreet's Business Web Factory system. Using that system, companies can connect on-the-fly with their partners and customers to achieve extended business reach and adapt to change almost faster than the speed of bytes – in *minutes* instead of months.

In a simple, hypothetical example, ''Federal Express has one core competency: they ship and track packages,'' Chazin says. ''Two years ago if I wanted to provide FedEx shipping on my Website, I'd have to call them and arrange to plug my Website into their back-end system, and they would have to do some development work to get my company on board. So a technological handshake had to occur before our companies could do business with each other.''

Through Bowstreet's plug-and-play business web technology, the need for that handshake – and the time and costs associated with it – has been eliminated. Using standard programming languages like XML, Bowstreet's system permits Web services to be automatically ''consumed'' by others online. Thus in the case of FedEx, information is transferred from the Website to FedEx's back-end system automatically. There are no humans involved (remember those?) directly in that process. The Website then automatically reformats the information for the screen so that customers can see when their product will ship, what the tracking number is, and other fine details about the transaction.

Now every major company has a Web services strategy. Microsoft is going so far as to break up its entire operating system into Web services, so that instead of downloading the entire Windows package, program components will be used as Web services online. Chazin says, "Web services are both evolutionary and revolutionary. They allow businesses to do things that they couldn't do before."

Walking the b-web talk

This is all very well and good, but does Bowstreet walk its b-web talk? After all, its mission is to "transform every business into a business web." Is Bowstreet transforming itself into a b-web? Indeed it is. In fact, Bowstreet's incremental evolution of its own b-web illustrates how a typical organization might transform itself into a b-web over time.

Chazin says "about a year ago we ran a project called Butterfly – for the metamorphosis of our company into a b-web as we emerge from our cocoon. And so we looked internally at all of the places where we could re-use assets across the company and leverage those assets both internally and externally. We started by gaining experience behind our own firewall before we opened it up to our partners and customers.

"We began by identifying all of the things that we were doing through internal paper systems. Then we looked for partners who specialize in those competencies so that we could build the front-end and plug directly into their systems. We now have what we call the Bowstreet Community Portal that allows employees to sign up for a learning course, order business cards, do Web-based conferencing, set up a conference call, sign purchase orders, etc.

"For example, in the past we had an internal conference call administrator, so we contracted with a company called Spiderphone. We now have a form we can fill out on our intranet to set up a conference call. It's integrated with our e-mail system, so it sends invitations to participants by e-mail. This can all be done over the Web and accessed from home, office, or while traveling as well. We leverage Spiderphone's competencies by plugging into their system.

"We do the same with purchase orders through eAlity. It's not our core competency to deal with that kind of stuff. All companies tend to outsource functions that are not their core strength. So you can literally build a virtual company easily and effectively through Web services in a way that could not have been done just two years ago.

"Coase's law is an economic principle that says primarily that a company will not outsource a function until it becomes cost effective for it to do so. If it's too expensive for you to outsource your HR function, you won't. However it's probably a very easy thing for you to outsource your payroll function, and about 80% of the companies in North America do so. That predated the Internet." The Internet makes it much easier to outsource, but until now each new contract required a lot of labor-intensive – and expensive – back-end development work by IT specialists. Bowstreet's technology exponentially reduces the technical and economic barriers to outsourcing and other forms of e-business partnering.

Once Bowstreet had successfully implemented its Community Portal behind the protection of its firewall, it began to open up the Portal to its customers and partners. "Now different customers from different client sites will log into the Bowstreet Community Portal and each will have a uniquely customized experience with access to different support materials," Chazin says. "So a potential customer who hasn't signed a purchase agreement with us yet might log into the Community Portal and see demos, marketing materials, etc. Once he's made a purchase, that same b-web, without any work on the part of the client, updates or morphs itself. That same client can now download the software he just purchased, the training materials he needs, sign up for courses, etc. As he purchases other options or moves to a different level, he automatically has access to more features through his self-morphing b-web – for example, the ability to chat live with a customer service rep, or take advantage of other premium services."

In a b-web, the boundaries that separate what is internal from what is external to an organization are increasingly blurred. For example, "that same Bowstreet Community Portal customer support center drives our center for external partners as well," Chazin explains. "Some of the services that we provide internally, like training and seminars, have been turned external, depending on who you are. It's all based on a set of profiles that changes the way the business web behaves when someone logs into it. It's that level of customization that had been prevented in the past, because you had to develop application-specific code for all of that.

"In the past, people built just one Website and tried to make changes within that one Website to satisfy different users. That became a code furball that IT had to deal with. Every time you had a new partner, IT would tear its hair out to accommodate the requests of business managers. That's where we've changed the economics of software. Our core competency is helping companies break through that barrier."

Business webs don't just happen. They've needed leading-edge technology that in one fell swoop demolishes both the economic and technical barriers to spontaneous e-lliance formation and dissolution. Bowstreet provides that leading-edge technology that makes b-webs happen. Better still, it walks its impressive b-web talk.

A brief history of Bowstreet

» **January 1998**: Former Tivoli chairman and CEO Frank Moss, and Preferred Systems co-founders Jack Serfass, David Sweet, and Joe Sommers founded Bowstreet, Inc.

» **March 1999**: In the first public use of the term *Web services*, Frank Moss said, "The shift to a Web services computing model will result in a fundamental change in the economics – and certainly the leadership – of the software industry."

» **July 1999**: Bowstreet, supported by IBM, Microsoft, Novell, Oracle and the Sun-Netscape Alliance, announced a specification for managing data about Web services, the Directory Services Markup Language (DSML).

» **August 1999**: Bob Crowley (formerly of Arbortext and Kenan Systems) joined as president and CEO.

» **November 1999**: Bowstreet announced the Bowstreet Business Web Factory, a platform for creating, combining, managing, deploying, and customizing Web services; Bowstreet also announced first customers.

» **2000**: Butterfly Project – metamorphosis into a b-web. Implemented Bowstreet Community Portal behind firewall.

> **November 2001**: Opened Bowstreet Community Portal to partners and customers.

THE THREAD WEAVES APPAREL INDUSTRY B-WEBS

Supply chains in the apparel industry come and go like trends in women's shoes. Designers, manufacturers, lenders, factories, inspectors, distributors, and shippers partner for a project, get the clothes out the door and disengage to embark on a new project. Every cycle results in new supply chains. Until now this dynamic making, breaking, and remaking of commercial relationships was at odds with e-commerce technology. The best available technology required months of programmers working overtime to connect partners and applications in an automated supply chain. It was too expensive and too time-consuming, so business just took place offline.

Yet analysts say the $200bn domestic apparel industry could save up to $34bn a year using automated Web connections through accelerated production cycle times, reduced mistakes, enhanced communication, and other supply chain efficiencies. So The Thread – an apparel industry sourcing hub founded by former executives of Liz Claiborne, The Limited Inc. and Warnaco – has found a way to lead that transformation with the help of its technology partner, Bowstreet, Inc. Now The Thread (www.thethread.com) is letting apparel industry companies come together on its Website, find new partners, create instant Web-based supply chains, execute projects and disband – as needed, all with a click of a mouse.

The apparel industry: challenges and opportunities

The fashion industry is huge by any standard, with European retail sales in 2000 estimated at $400bn and US apparel-only figures exceeding $200bn. World-wide estimates range from $800bn at retail to well over $1trn. The industry is highly fragmented and consists of retailers, manufacturers, wholesalers, importers, raw material suppliers, foreign procurement agents, and factories.

In the apparel industry, designing a garment, producing it in large quantities, and delivering it to the racks of thousands of retail outlets world-wide requires collaboration and synchronization of numerous processes inside dozens of companies. For example, a manufacturer based in the United States may receive an order for several thousand units of a sweater from a designer. Besides the design specifications, the order typically includes the different sizes required, colors, delivery dates, and shipping instructions. The manufacturer may contract the production to several factories in Thailand and source the fabric and trim from suppliers in Egypt and China.

At the same time, several related activities are also taking place. These include issuing letters of credit, payments, tests, quality control checks, inspections, and checks to insure that international trade regulations and country import quotas are not being violated. Successful completion of the project requires the co-ordination and synchronization of hundreds of processes across all participating organizations.

Poor communications

These extraordinary co-ordination challenges have been exacerbated by "poor communications up and down the supply chain," says Haim Dabah, founder of The Thread, thereby "delaying effective production and slowing deliveries to stores. This industry is fragmented and has no standards. It works with spreadsheets, late-night phone calls, faxes you can't read. Even the best of the best conduct business this way."

Gene Ostrovsky, executive VP of operations for The Thread, concurs. "Up until this point, the apparel industry has depended upon traditional person-to-person communication, with no meaningful automation to speak of. There's been little sense of security that all the pieces will come together to enable projects to complete on time and within budget."

Excessive wastage

Consulting studies have found that soft goods supply chains contain as much as 83% of non-value-adding processes. These significant inefficiencies are primarily due to the lack of timely, reliable information, and a need to cover subsequent poor decision-making. Supply chain waste mainly manifests itself in excess inventories, higher cost of goods and processes, and longer product fulfilment cycles.

Further, "apparel happens to be one of the most wasteful supply chains," Ostrovsky explains, "because it is extremely fragmented, and because the industry has been notoriously phobic toward any kind of standardization or automation. There are very few automation success stories in the apparel industry. In addition, there are no clearly dominant entities in this industry. The biggest manufacturer controls maybe 3% of the market.

"The entire apparel industry supply chain is roughly nine to twelve months long from concept to delivery. Only about a third of that time is spent adding value to product, with about six to nine months wasted. So the opportunity is tremendous. And apparel is very fashion-conscious, so the more you can shorten that time, the better. You can hit the season right on the nose."

Retailers typically place orders with apparel contractors many months in advance of the delivery date. From that point on, however, there has been no "visibility into the progression of that merchandise through the supply chain until it shows up on the delivery date," Ostrovsky says. "And if it doesn't show up or if it shows up late, it's too late to do anything about it. The cost of not knowing where your product is in every step through the supply chain is tremendous. So there was and is a great need for a product which allows both retailers and manufacturers the visibility into this 'black hole' of product fulfilment."

For many years software companies attempted to streamline discrete supply chains by applying rigid client/server technologies to manage very dynamic and custom processes. The success of such technologies was largely predicated upon an organization's ability to alter its processes to conform to best practices embedded into a particular technology.

However, in the apparel industry, most process automation efforts failed. It became obvious over time that this highly-fragmented industry, with virtually non-existent standards and literally thousands of custom supply chains, would be strongly resistant to change. It also became clear that for any technology solution to succeed in such a flexibility-hungry environment, it has to be able to change and adjust rapidly to the unique processes and culture of every participating company, rather than futilely trying to change all of those cultures to fit the technology.

The solution

Thus The Thread's main business challenge was to develop a flexible collaboration framework that could easily be adopted by *any* manufacturer, supplier, or service provider in the apparel industry. The solution would have to allow different companies to plug-and-play with minimal effort and without having to request system management and support services from The Thread to initiate assembly and disassembly of business webs. Additionally, the solution had to be business-driven – giving production managers access to critical information no matter where their companies are in the supply chain.

The Thread set out to streamline many of the tasks in the apparel industry. It began by spending several months mapping out the business processes currently in use in the apparel, footwear, fashion manufacturing, and sourcing businesses. They "took the apparel supply chain and broke it up into a bunch of functional 'units,'" Ostrovsky explains. "Examples include a 'lab dip,' which is a process of approving the desired color for a fabric, and a 'sample process,' which involves obtaining product samples."

They found that the business processes and practices in use varied wildly. They also noticed that most of the buyers were based in the US, Canada, Europe, or Japan (80%+), most of the sellers (factories, agents) resided in emerging markets, and the raw materials producers were spread throughout. They also studied many notable failures in automation within this industry and found that most of them were due to inflexibility in dealing with all of the variables.

In order to build the needed level of flexibility into its solution, The Thread broke the apparel supply chain into about 200 of those individual functional units. It then created individual Web services out of those units. "Keep in mind that the Web services do not correspond to a particular player, they correspond to a process," Ostrovsky says. "We are general enough in the dissection of the supply chain to allow all potential apparel industry participants to play. The Web service and Bowstreet's software give our users infinite ability to modify this

Web service to their own specifications *without any programing whatsoever*, just by modifying templates and profiles. A collection of these Web services can then be strung together like a string of pearls to create a custom supply chain. That's how we achieved the flexibility of the software.''

The Thread, which went live early in 2001, extends participating companies' market reach while reducing their risk and transaction costs. The Thread continuously tracks and reports performance on all partners and processes using the service. Partners in these automated supply chains share back-end information such as order status, on-time performance metrics, shipping schedules, budgets, and much more. The beauty of the system is that users get infinitely customized views of their supply chains and the processes involved.

These combinations of Web services replace the monolithic, hard-coded Websites that took too much time and money to build in the past (when they were built at all). As The Thread participants create private supply chains, each user within each company sees *individually-customized menus* of his apparel projects, factories, and partners, along with performance scorecards, customizable reports, and virtual office tools.

Now "many partners can participate in different stages of the supply chain simultaneously," Ostrovsky says, "and they can all operate and work off of the same set of real-time information. Instead of each participant in the supply chain waiting to begin his task until his predecessor has completed his responsibility, they collaborate on the particular task together in real time. So it's not a hand-off. They achieve better results, and make better decisions, faster." This results in the shortening of lead times.

Steve Chazin at Bowstreet notes "The Thread is an exceptional example of a business web in action. They are the first ones that are dipping their toes into building a truly virtual corporation. They are solving a problem that has heretofore been unsolvable. They've made it possible for all of the partners involved in building a line of clothing to come together at one place at one time by simply plugging into The Thread's b-web infrastructure. Each participant adds value, contributes his core competencies, and does what he does best, all within transient, fully-customizable business webs.

"The Thread can also use the same framework or model and customize it for the next project. So supply chains disband, but the same framework can be used to pull together for the next project; it's the kind of plugging and unplugging that allows these business webs to form. Building one product for one designer line for one season is very different from one season to another, but the *process* is the same."

Roll out the b-webs – and let the savings begin!

Leo Massarani, chief technology officer for The Thread, estimates that without Bowstreet technology this application would have taken twice as long to build and four times the resources to achieve only 50% of its flexibility and configurability. "We'd have had no choice other than to hardcode fixed business processes, and suffer through slower adoption," Massarani said. "We believe that we saved approximately $4mn as a result."

Massarani also estimates that adding each new partner to its b-web would have required 5000 man-hours of effort, and these man-hours of work would have to have been supplied by expensive IT consultants. With The Thread's Private Supply Chain software running on Bowstreet's Business Web Factory, Massarani estimates that the amount of time required to add a new partner is just 60 hours – that's just over 1% of 5000! Those 60 hours includes training and consulting time as well as the time required to configure and customize the application. Thus at an average estimated consulting rate of $180/hour, the Bowstreet Business Web Factory saves nearly $900,000 in consulting costs for each partner that The Thread adds.

Now supply-chain participants are reducing wastage dramatically and reaping big rewards. For example, "one $100mn company cut their costs by $1mn," Ostrovsky says, "with most of the savings in areas such as travel, air freight, phone, fax, and FedEx."

Even with these successes, however, Ostrovsky notes that, due to the historically technophobic nature of the apparel industry, "it's not an immediate sale. It takes demonstration and discussion. But it's also important to point out that the industry is rapidly becoming familiar with technology, and retailers are getting more and more involved in the fulfilment cycle. As they do, it's becoming survival of the fittest, whereas it didn't always work that way."

"We're basically transforming the apparel industry into business webs, where companies focus on their core competencies, partner for a project, then reformulate for the next one," The Thread's CEO Bill Anderson says. "The Internet, like us, becomes much more than a communications tool or alternate sales channel. It's the business itself, the common thread."

"Other companies are building webs to solve finite problems," says Bowstreet's Steve Chazin. "This gives us a sneak peek into the future into what we think all companies will begin to be able to do."

> **Major milestones in the life of The Thread**
> » **First quarter of 1999**: client-server prototype developed.
> » **January 2000**: The Thread was launched.
> » **August 2000**: initial proof of Private Supply Chain (PSC) concept completed.
> » **November 2000**: PSC R1.0 specification completed.
> » **January 2001**: PSC R1.0 released to pilot customers.
> » **April 2001**: PSC released.

INCUBATING WORKER DEMOCRACIES: THE MONDRAGON MODEL

One of the primary trends in organizational models of the past several decades has been away from command-and-control, highly-centralized, hierarchical decision-making, toward increasingly decentralized, more participative models. Even so, few go so far as to advocate the complete democratization of business organizations. Democratic organization represents the most radical extension of this movement toward increasing participation. This is ironic, given the relative triumph of democracy in so many nation states around the world. We live in societies that are more or less democratic, yet we spend the great majority of our lives living and working inside organizations that are not.

Many in business may scoff at the idea of democratic organization as quaint or simply impractical. After all, collaborative decision-making is notoriously slow and cumbersome.[1] Yet co-operative organizations in many countries exemplify the efficacy and potential of worker democracies. The Mondragon co-operatives in the Basque region of Spain are perhaps the best-known example, with more than 70 books and 60 journal articles published regarding various aspects of them.[2]

Since its humble beginnings in 1956, Mondragon has grown from a five-member manufacturing co-operative start-up to a complex of dozens of co-operatives in a range of services and industries. Together they employ more than 30,000 people in a variety of countries. Mondragon's annual revenues of US $5bn rival many Fortune 500 companies (see table below). And this has all been accomplished within "a unique worker democracy in which the employees own the enterprises, the capital/worker relationship has been inverted, and entrepreneurship flourishes at a rate of success unparalleled anywhere else in the world."[3] Mondragon's extensive history is briefly summarized in the following table for those who may not be familiar with it.

A brief history of Mondragon[2,4,5,6,7,8]

» **1930s:** Franco deposed Spanish democratic coalition government. Basque country remained an anti-fascist stronghold.
» **1941:** Father José Maria Arizmendiarrieta came to Mondragon parish and found the town devastated by Spanish Civil War. Started vocational school.
» **1956:** Five of school's graduates became engineers. They launched the first co-operative, Fagor, which manufactured kerosene cookers.
» **1958:** Mondragon co-ops employed 149 workers; Spanish government said co-op members were not eligible for social security or unemployment benefits; co-op created its own, less expensive social security system; that system provided seed money for co-op to start its own bank.
» **1973:** 10,000 workers employed.
» **1976:** 14,665 workers employed in 65 Mondragon co-operatives; exports represented 10% of total production.
» **1986:** Under the bank's leadership, Mondragon launched 103 co-ops since 1956: only 3 failed; Spain joined European Economic Community; this opened up new competitive environment for

Mondragon, which stopped creating new co-ops and channeled its resources into expanding its existing companies in order to compete.

» **1988**: Mondragon managers' meeting: *Facing Up to the European Community*.

» **1990**: 21,241 member employees; Mondragon Cooperative Corporation (MCC) was formed to centralize and speed up decision-making; leadership shifted from the bank to MCC.

» **1990s**: annual increases in financial strength, investments, and pay levels.

» **1997**: 34,400 employed; exports were 46.1% of total production (up from 10% in 1976).

» **2000**: MCC was Spain's eighth largest corporation and was *twice as profitable* as any other Spanish corporation, ranking ahead of Fortune 500 companies like Owens-Corning; MCC's annual revenues US $5bn; MCC's bank administers more than US $5bn annually; rated among the 100 most efficient financial institutions in the world in terms of profit/asset ratio.

A tale of two Mondragons

The forces of globalization split the history of Mondragon's evolution in two. The transition began with Spain's entry into the European Economic Community in 1986, which led to the formation of the Mondragon Co-operative Corporation (MCC) in 1990 and its assumption of leadership from Mondragon's co-operative bank, Caja Laboral.

Mondragon no. 1

During its first 30, pre-globalization, years under the leadership of Caja Laboral, Mondragon became a thriving incubator for successful worker democracies. During that period it launched 103 co-operatives; only three of which closed. That translates into an entrepreneurial success rate of 80%, roughly equal to the failure rate in the rest of the world.[2] "This is particularly impressive when you consider that the Basque region lost well over 100,000 jobs during Spain's deep 10-year recession that started in 1975. During that difficult time Mondragon co-ops actually added workers."[5]

Mondragon no. 2

In the last decade, Mondragon has strayed to some extent from the democratic principles that are at the heart of the co-operative movement in order to meet the competitive challenges of globalization posed by Spain's entry into the European Economic Community. That entry ended the relative isolation of the Basque region that had nurtured Mondragon's development. It was uncertain whether Mondragon would fare as well if it were to become a co-operative democratic island immersed in a hyper-competitive capitalistic world.

In order to compete with multinationals, "the co-ops adopted characteristics of their rivals . . . they needed a quick, centralized system of decision-making to compete in a rapidly changing and complex global market. So by 1990 co-op leaders formed the . . . MCC. MCC operates in a much more centralized manner than the co-op complex had under the bank's leadership. Its management structure makes important decisions on, and co-ordinates, distribution and marketing for all three types of co-operative enterprise – financial, industrial, and retail/distribution."[3]

George Cheney, author of *Values at Work: Employee Participation Meets Market Pressure at Mondragon*,[6] notes the impact that these changes have had on the social values that have been so central to Mondragon. For example, and perhaps not surprisingly, "more hierarchical distance is perceived and complained of by workers now, calling into question the key value of equality."[7] In addition, workers feel that the scope of their decision-making has narrowed. Previously they had been involved in all significant organizational decisions, but now they primarily make job-related decisions in order to please customers. "In the face of market pressures, participation was demanded from employees rather than viewed as their natural right as organization participants."[7]

In its efforts to globalize effectively, MCC embarked on other controversial initiatives, including becoming (in the eyes of some critical observers), "a traditional capitalist employer operating its own plants in low-wage countries like Egypt, Morocco, Mexico, Argentina, Thailand, and China. Its employees in these countries are not co-op members.

But even within Spain, MCC developed non-co-op businesses, many as joint ventures with capitalist partners, and has been using an increasing number of non-member workers within its core co-ops as well. Now about one-third of Mondragon workers are non-members, far exceeding the original Mondragon commitment to never employ more than 10% non-members. The managers justify this change by arguing that the increased volatility of the global market requires a more dispensable sector of the workforce."[3] Given the increasing percentage of contract workers, MCC is mirroring the corporate trend toward achieving flexibility via a shamrock organizational model (see Chapter 8), which consists of a core staff supported by both full-time and part-time or intermittent contract workers.

Principles of Mondragon's success

Although MCC's approach to globalization has been at odds with some of Mondragon's core social values, MCC has succeeded in its goal of becoming a thriving global competitor (clearly demonstrated in the year 2000 highlights in table above). And even though decision-making has been centralized in MCC, members still have the ability to vote out its board. Further, MCC "is doing an extraordinary job of creating new employment – including jobs in manufacturing. The MCC has found ways to advance in high technology fields while still maintaining a strong presence in manufacturing."[1]

Noted futurist, author, and business thinker Joel Barker identifies five principles that underlie the continuing success of MCC.[2]

1 **Democratic power structure**: Every MCC member has a vote. They elect MCC's board of directors, which in turn hires its managers. So workers have the ability to replace their board if they're not satisfied with management. Other democratic structures include a council of workers that oversees upper management, and a representative social council.

2 **Financial structures**: First, all MCC members are required to invest some of their own money in the co-operative that they work for. They are unable to access that money until retirement. So all members have a financial interest in the long-term performance of the organization that they work for. Second, the co-operative bank "risks its capital to

protect the job base of the community", and catalyzes the creation of new co-operative businesses. Third, MCC is self-insured against unemployment, and it has a deep commitment to creating and protecting jobs. Therefore it goes to great lengths to prevent job loss. For example, in an effort to retain jobs it reduces all wages to 80% in struggling co-operatives, transfers workers from them to other healthy co-operatives, and provides immediate retraining for workers who become unemployed (and very few have in all of Mondragon's long history).

3 **Education linked to co-operative needs**: Graduates of Father José's vocational school started its first co-op. Over the year's the school's curriculum expanded to meet the needs of the growing co-operatives. The school is "now considered one of the best business schools in all of Europe".

4 **Fair pay**: Mondragon succeeded in capping its pay ratio at 6:1 (highest:lowest paid) during its first three decades. Even today that ratio has only risen to 15:1 (as opposed to a whopping 115:1 in major US corporations in 1996) in order to help retain Mondragon's highly sought-after managerial talent.

5 **Equitable retirement plan**: As noted in the table above, Mondragon created its own retirement fund in 1958 when the Spanish government said that co-op members were not eligible for social security or unemployment benefits. Mondragon's plan was actually less costly for its members than was the government's. Members now contribute about 32% of their earnings to the plan, and their benefits amount to 60% of their final pay level, plus a vegetable garden plot on their retirement if they don't already have one.

Mondragon is not alone

Mondragon may be the most famous example of democratic co-operatives, but it is by no means the only one. For example, "the Italian co-op movement is even larger than the Basque, with about 250,000 worker co-op members alone. They also have taken advantage of their labor flexibility and dedication to quality work to serve the new niche markets created by the volatile global market. Rapid technological change and the move toward just-in-time delivery systems have created a demand for small orders of customized industrial parts. Small to medium-sized manufacturers with highly skilled workforces band together in 'flexible manufacturing networks.' While capitalist businesses also can do this, co-ops that manage to build collaborative cultures are even better able to foster the mutual relationships required for networks to work."[3]

Mondragon, and the world-wide co-operative movement that it exemplifies, successfully reverses "one of the most important premises of capitalism," Barker says. "The old rule of business is: *when you are faced with the choice of risking your capital to protect jobs or risking jobs to protect your capital, always protect your capital*."[3] As noted above, however, Mondragon, through its culture and all of its institutions, strives to generate and protect its jobs. Layoffs are a last resort. "Why such a concern about co-operative membership and job creation? In the context of US-style private enterprise management, there would be no concern about job creation. In the United States, a large layoff is often followed by a rise in the company's stock value, suggesting that many US managers look upon workers as a cost, disregarding their value to the enterprise."[2] Mondragon shines as a thriving, successful beacon of possibility in a world grown cynical with empty corporate slogans that trumpet "our people are our greatest asset," while thousands of those same people are surgically eliminated at the first sign of a significant market downturn or corporate restructuring.

Before Father José Maria Arizmendiarrieta died in 1976, two decades after the birth of Mondragon, he wrote, "hand in hand, of one mind, renewed, united in work, through work, in our small land we shall create a more human environment for everyone and we shall improve this land. We shall include villages and towns in our new equality; the people and everything else: 'Ever Forward.'"[8]

KEY LEARNING POINTS
Bowstreet and b-webs

» **Web services** are the essential building blocks of business webs. They represent digitized core competencies that businesses can leverage both internally and externally.

» **Business webs** are made possible by the Internet, but transaction costs remained relatively high until the development of plug-and-play business web technology like the Bowstreet Business Web Factory.

» **Dissagregation** of previously internalized organizational competencies – and the structures associated with them – is likely to rev up to warp speed and transform our rapidly-antiquated twentieth-century models of organization.

» **Brave new models** will emerge. Not just variations on trends in progress like the hollowing out of organizations through outsourcing, but business models that were not possible – and even unthinkable – previously. The case of The Thread provides a glimpse of the tremendous possibilities that lie ahead – expressed in the form of a b-web that is happening now, and that spawns an infinite variety of transient b-webs.

The Thread and b-webs in the apparel industry

» **Web services** represent identifiable, relatively discrete processes. They do not refer to individual companies that execute those processes.

» **Dissagregation** of hierarchical organizations is not required in the apparel industry because that industry is already highly fragmented into of thousands upon thousands of small companies around the world. Typically each of those small companies specializes in one or at most a few supply-chain processes.

» **Contracts and agreements** characterize the majority of apparel industry b-web relationships. This places them closest to the markets end of the continuum of collaborative forms (see Chapter 6). As such, these collaborative relationships are at the lower end of the interdependence scale. Such relationships are more readily amenable to facilitation through plug-and-play b-web technology. However, the technology is also capable of supporting more complex, interdependent collaborative relationships. And keep in mind that the technology and the possibilities that it offers are still in their infancy, and will continue to expand over time.

» **Huge savings** – and profits – are in store for The Thread and all supply-chain participants. Even though The Thread's Private

Supply Chain was just launched in April 2001, participants have already begun to reap big rewards.

» **Technology now adapts** to organizational cultures. For the past two decades it has been mostly the other way around. This is nothing short of miraculous! A fully-customizable, Web-enabled, collaborative supply-chain software that cranks out fleeting apparel industry b-webs. But does it make coffee?

Mondragon and worker democracies

» **The world's most successful incubator** existed long before Silicon Valley. This holistic, democratic, worker-owner model generates far more than profits. It nurtures the generation and sustenance of vital, healthy businesses and communities.

» **Workplace democracy and ownership** offer "real and viable alternatives to the stockholder paradigm," and to the common corporate practice of significantly constraining, controlling, and otherwise managing employees' voice and power.

» **Shared vision and values** can provide a powerful alternative to command-and-control hierarchy (see Chapter 6).

» **Protecting jobs** can, with the right culture and supports, be a top priority and contribute to long-term growth and financial success.

» **Education + social values and vision + bank = long-term community job base**, especially when all are committed to job formation instead of capital formation.

» **Mondragon redefines success** as being "how many more quality jobs can be added than in the previous year, ... how much more education might be provided, how much more advanced can its technology applications become, how much greater can its attention to innovation become, or what innovations can advance its already premier banking and finance development. MCC co-operativists have excelled economically and politically by emphasizing their sense of social ethics, as well as their sense of workplace ethics, to bring work and society together, by cultivating a company of companies for a community of communities."

» **Business, politics, and community** "MCC teaches us that human creativity and dignity can be intertwined with economic and community well-being. Economic abstractions undermine opportunities to understand the relationship between work, people, and communities, and workers can become confused about how to take care of each other's needs. Such abstractions can also undermine people's ability to use their political system to exercise vigilance over their economic system."

» **Our models shape our world** and what we perceive as possible. They influence the design of all of our institutions, and liberate or suppress human ingenuity, dignity, vitality, and voice.

NOTES

1 Fitzgerald, S.P. (2002) *Decision Making*. Capstone Publishing Ltd, UK.

2 White, W.F. (1999) "The Mondragon co-operatives in 1976 and 1998." *Industrial & Labor Relations Review*, April [Ithaca].

3 Barker, J.A. (1997) "The Mondragon model: a new pathway for the twenty-first century." In: Hesselbein, F., Goldsmith, M., & Beck-hard, R. (eds) (1997) *The Organization of the Future*. Drucker Foundation Future Series, Jossey-Bass Publishers, San Francisco.

4 Schweickart, D. (1998) "The myth of Mondragon: co-operatives, politics, and working-class life in a Basque town." *Science & Society,* Winter issue [New York].

5 Huet, T. (1997) "Can co-ops go global? Mondragon is trying," *Dollars & Sense*, November/December.

6 Cheney, G. (1999) *Values at Work: Employee Participation Meets Market Pressure at Mondragon*. Cornell University Press, Ithaca, NY.

7 Meyer, J. (2001) "Values at work: employee participation meets market pressure at Mondragon." *The Southern Communication Journal,* Winter issue [Memphis, TN].

8 Abascal-Hildebrand, M. (2000) "Mondragon's algebra of community economics." *Peace Review*, June [Palo Alto, CA].

Key Concepts and Thinkers in Organizational Models

This chapter provides additional information on key thinkers in the area of organizational and business models, brief descriptions of more organizational models and metaphors, and descriptions of several related concepts, including downsizing, business process re-engineering, and outsourcing.

This chapter provides background information on a few key thinkers in the area of organizational and business models, followed by brief descriptions of even more models and metaphors, and concludes with definitions of several related expressions. The listings are intended to provide a diverse, representative overview, but are by no means comprehensive.

A FEW KEY THINKERS

Warren Bennis – Distinguished professor of Business Administration at the Marshall School, and founding chairman of the Leadership Institute at the University of Southern California. He is the author of 26 books on leadership, including the best-selling *Leaders* and *On Becoming a Leader*, both translated into 21 languages. He has also acted as a consultant for many Fortune 500 companies, and advised four US presidents. In 1996 he proclaimed the death of bureaucracy.[1]

Charles Handy – An independent writer, educator, and social philosopher. He is a consultant to a wide variety of organizations in business, government, healthcare, and education. Formerly a professor at the London Business School for many years, and a first-class graduate of Oxford University, he also holds honorary doctorates from four British universities. Many in the UK know him for his "Thoughts for Today" on the BBC's radio show *Today*. He is the author of several highly-regarded books, and conceived the *Shamrock* and *Membership Communities* organizational models described below. His main concern is the implication for society of the dramatic changes that technology and economics are bringing to the workplace and to all our lives. (A brief biography is available at www.ic.siemens.com/CDA/Site/GHTML/box/1,1562,5306-1-0,00.html).

Dee Hock – Founder and CEO emeritus of VISA USA and VISA International. In 1991 he was recognized as one of 30 living laureates of the Business Hall of Fame for his innovations in management and organization. In 1992 he was cited as one of eight people who most changed our way of life in the last quarter century. He is the founder and CEO of The Chaordic Alliance, whose purpose is to create "the conditions for the formation of practical, innovative organizations that blend competition and co-operation to address critical societal issues" (www.chaordic.org). (A brief biography is available at www.odnetwork.org/confgallery/deehockbio.html).

Henry Mintzberg – John Cleghorn professor of Management Studies at McGill University in Montreal. He is one of the great thinkers and writers on organizations, particularly in the area of strategy. His extensive publications include *The Rise and Fall of Strategic Planning*, which won the Academy of Management's best book award in 1995. He identified five generic forms of organizational models: simple structure, machine bureaucracy, professional bureaucracy, divisionalized form, and adhocracy.[2]

Gareth Morgan – A distinguished research professor at the Schulich School of Business, York University, Toronto, he has been elected Life Fellow of the International Academy of Management in recognition of an outstanding international contribution to the science and art of management. His books include *Images of Organization* (on organizational metaphors, some of which are defined briefly below,) *Riding the Waves of Change*, and *Imaginization: The Art of Creative Management*. (See www.yorku.ca/faculty/academic/gmorgan for more information).

Herbert A. Simon – (1916–2001) Beginning in the 1940s, Simon advocated a contingency approach to organizational models as an alternative to the mechanistic and humanistic models that vied for dominance in the first half of the twentieth century. Contingency models did not take root, however, until the late 1960s. (An autobiography is available at www.nobel.se/economics/laureates/1978/simon-autobio.html).

Don Tapscott – An internationally-sought authority, consultant and speaker on business strategy and organizational transformation. His clients include top executives of many of the world's largest corporations, and government leaders from many countries. The Washington Technology Report says he is one of the most influential media authorities since Marshall McLuhan. He has authored or co-authored seven widely-read books on the application of technology in business, including *Digital Capital*, which describes how business webs are replacing the traditional model of the firm and changing the dynamics of wealth creation and competition (www.dontapscott.com).

Max Weber – (1864–1920) This German sociologist developed a model of an "ideal" bureaucracy that includes distinct characteristics like division of labor, hierarchy, impersonality, codified rules and regulations, promotion based on achievement, goal orientation, and efficiency. His research on bureaucracies is the foundation of organizational sociology (www.faculty.rsu.edu/~felwell/Theorists/Weber/Whome.htm#).

EVEN MORE MODELS AND METAPHORS

Amoebas – These grow fast and split instinctively when they feel they are beginning to lose touch with their customers. They also have strong instincts of customer-orientation and innovation. People in these organizations are motivated by the chance to run their own show. Empowerment is built into the structures and systems. Amoebas may also be characterized by disorganized systems, especially around the soft issues of management as they rarely stand still for long enough to put these in order. Typical amoeba organizations include young, entrepreneurial high-technology companies.

Boundaryless organizations – These have abandoned the attempt to maintain the distinction between their operations and those of their suppliers and customers. They operate through networks of expert sub-contractors, mostly smaller businesses than themselves, or self-employed freelancers. They enter into joint ventures with customers and freely second their own staff to customers' organizations. They retain their identity by remaining within a clearly defined market niche and venturing outside that niche only in partnerships with other similar organizations. Typical boundaryless organizations are specialist management consultancies. Their culture is pragmatic, strongly individualistic, and heavily reliant on relationships.

Brain – Brain as organization has become a dominant metaphor that has given rise to views of organization as information-processing and learning systems. The current focus on "learning organizations" is a manifestation of the organization-as-brain metaphor. In his insightful chapter on organizations as brains, Gareth Morgan explores the contributions that various images of the brain, cybernetics, and principles of holographic design make toward the development of this metaphor. Morgan identifies the principles of holographic organizational design as being:

» "get the whole into the parts;
» create connectivity and redundancy;
» create simultaneous specialization and generalization; and
» create a capacity to self-organize."[5]

Business webs or b-webs – Canadian high-tech guru Don Tapscott celebrates the arrival of "a new business form" (really a souped-up virtual organization) which is made up of "fluid congregations of businesses sometimes highly structured, sometimes amorphous, that come together on the Internet to create value for customers and wealth for their shareholders." Tapscott labels this new form a "business web" or "b-web." Business webs are a "universal business platform" made up of "a distinct system of suppliers, distributors, commerce services providers, infrastructure providers and customers."

Chemical soup organizations – These differ from boundaryless organizations in that while the latter have a clear framework of fixed structures and reporting lines in which people find their own freedom to operate, the chemical soup organization often appears to have no fixed structures at all. The main driving force, outside of the senior management vision, is a motley collection of ever-changing project teams. Chemical soups are often relatively large organizations, going through rapid growth or cultural transformation.

Instruments of domination – These represent the ugly aspects of organizations and the view that our organizations are in fact killing us through domination; exploitation based on class, race, gender; environmental and social degradation; occupational hazards; disease; accidents and death; promotion of workaholism; excessive mental stress; and multinational imperialism.[5] Downsizing (see below) may also be viewed as an expression of this metaphor, as can the 1996 book, *Corporate Abuse.*[3]

Knowledge cafés – These are among the new breed of organizational models, according to business writer Leif Edvinsson.[4] After all, where does the exchange of ideas work best? The kitchen or the boardroom? The relaxed atmosphere of the kitchen or any similar space is more conducive to the kind of thinking and behavior required of modern managers and organizations. For example, Skandia's office in Vienna includes a Viennese-style café to encourage cultural bonding between employees from various nationalities.

Groups of up to 1000 have been involved in "café learning conversations" on issues ranging from fostering treaty negotiations with Maori leaders in New Zealand to scenario planning in Mexico. Variations on the original café idea model now include Passion Café, Story Café, and Friday Café. All take the format and atmosphere of a café to foster and nurture discussion. They may be used within existing organizations, or to form temporary learning organizations.

Membership communities – These are an extension of Handy's shamrock model (see below). With this model Handy suggests that successful organizations of the future will be what he calls "membership communities." In order to hold people to an organization which can no longer promise them a job for life, companies have to offer some other form of continuity and sense of belonging. To do this, he suggests, companies have to imbue members with certain rights. The notion is similar to that of a federal organization, built on the principle of subsidiarity. The center is kept small and its primary purpose is to be "in charge of the future."

Organism – This became one of the most common organizational metaphors in the last century, second only to the machine metaphor. It has led to "many of the most important developments in organization theory over the last 50 years."[5] Those developments include thinking of organizations as open systems (see Chapter 2) interacting with and dependent upon the environments in which they live for their nourishment and survival. It is also includes contingency theories of adapting organizations to fit their environments, organizational needs, growth, health, and development, and identifying and classifying different "species" or types of organizations, like amoebas (see above).

Psychic prisons – This metaphor is based on the realization that organizations, in fact, exist primarily as psychic phenomena. You cannot see, feel, taste, or touch organizations. Although there is physical evidence of their existence (e.g., their by-products and artefacts), they are essentially "created and sustained by conscious and unconscious processes, with the notion that people can actually become imprisoned or confined by the images, ideas, thoughts, and actions to which these processes give rise."[5] Further, we tend to give these mental creations "an existence and power of their own that allow them to exercise a measure of control" over us. In his provocative chapter on organizations as psychic prisons, Gareth Morgan[5] explores the murky waters of the unconscious including the role of repressed sexuality, patriarchal family, death and immortality, anxiety, shadow, archetype, and dolls and teddy bears in organizational images and life.

Shamrock organizations - These were first envisioned by management writer Charles Handy[6] to describe a type of organizational structure with three parts or leaves. The first leaf of the shamrock represents the core staff of the organization. The second leaf consists of the contractual fringe, which may consist of individuals and other organizations, and often includes people who once worked for the organization but now provide it with services. The third leaf includes the flexible labor force. More than simply hired hands, these workers have to be sufficiently close to the organization to feel a sense of commitment which ensures that their work, although part-time or intermittent, is carried out to a high standard. Handy's model, or some variation of it, is often used to explain the move to outsourcing non-core functions.

Stars - These are built around a small number of large customers. Everything they do mirrors a customer need. They may operate from the customer's premises and may even have absorbed some of the customer's former staff. The majority of people in the organization are concerned with delivery and they are supported by a relatively small core of experts and administrative staff. The pace is partially or wholly dictated by that of the customer, although part of the customer expectation may be that the star organization stimulates the cultural and technical innovation that its own people cannot. Typical star organizations would be IT contractors such as Perot Systems or the FI Group.

Virtual organizations - Much beloved of management theorists, these have more than one interpretation. To some people, the virtual concept refers simply to the ability of companies to use IT to allow people in different locations, and even on different continents, to work together effectively. Others regard this as simply the beginning. A number of companies have found that virtual working allows the traditional structure of the organization to be discarded altogether. They advocate an organizational model which can bring together individuals or companies to work on a single project, where the virtual organization or team exists only for as long as it is required to complete the project and is then disbanded. The virtual organization model significantly predates the business web model, yet they are essentially identical. The b-web virtual organization is made possible by recent technological advances (see Chapters 4, 5, and 7 for additional information and cases).

RELATED CONCEPTS

Downsizing – The term *downsizing* was coined by the American management academic Stephen Roach. He advocated a wholesale reduction in staffing levels as the key to greater efficiency. Originally intended as the antidote to the growing bureaucracy within large American organizations, downsizing became and unfortunately continues to be a flag of convenience for many organizations looking to reduce costs by cutting headcount.

In many cases, downsizing and delayering have been pursued with such vigor and disregard for the human cost that its victims and survivors alike have come to regard it as little more than a cynical exercise. Confronted by the unpalatable face of capitalism, even Roach himself has since recanted, claiming that many companies took downsizing too far and used it for the wrong purposes. Nevertheless, the practice has become stubbornly entrenched in manager's toolkits as a quick-fix cost-cutting strategy.

Business process re-engineering (BPR) – This is allied to the downsizing trend. BPR has been one of the most significant influences on management thinking in the past decade. As described in *The Business Magazine*, BPR "involves fundamentally rethinking and redesigning the processes, which we often take for granted, in order to achieve dramatic improvements in business performance." It requires managers to map and analyze core processes in detail, from beginning (for example, R&D) to end (e.g. final delivery to the customer). Departmental barriers are ignored in the exercise;

it is the process that counts. The idea is to create a much simpler process, with fewer layers of management and a radically different organizational structure.

It is far from revolutionary, however. Many commentators have observed that re-engineering was simply a logical next step following on from scientific management (Taylorism), industrial engineering, and business process improvement (total quality management, or TQM). What re-engineering had going for it, though, was that it fitted the needs of companies looking for a reason to continue the attack on traditional bureaucratic, hierarchical structures.

Outsourcing – This involves contracting with external vendors for non-core services that had previously been performed by departments or functions within the organization. "Most outsourcing decisions are based on the relative efficiency of buying products and services *versus* producing them in-house. The more an organization outsources its work, the more it depends on market transactions with external organizations."[7] A great majority of American companies, for example, outsource their payroll function. Duplicating, catering, and IT functions are also increasingly outsourced. The concept of outsourcing is integral to several organizational models, including the shamrock, hollowed-out,[8] virtual, and business web models.

NOTES

1 Bennis, W.G. (1996) "The coming death of bureaucracy." *Think*, November/December.

2 Mintzberg, H. (1981) "Organization design: fashion or fit?" *Harvard Business Review*, (January/February).

3 Wright, L. & Smye, M. (1996) *Corporate Abuse*. MacMillan, New York.

4 Edvinsson, L. (2002) *Corporate Longitude*. FT/Prentice Hall, London.

5 Morgan, G. (1986) *Images of Organization*. Sage, Beverly Hills, CA.

6 Handy, C. (1998) *The Age of Unreason*. Harvard Business School Press, Boston, MA.

7 Robey, D. & Sales, C.A. (1994) *Designing Organizations*, 4th edn. Irwin, Burr Ridge, IL.

8 Heller, R. (1993) "The dangers of econstruction." *Management Today*.

Resources for Organizational Models

Today the Web provides ready access to an increasing variety of high quality information and resources related to business and organizational models. This chapter provides descriptions of and links to Web-based knowledge portals, cases, interviews, online courses, white papers, and additional information on a selection of organizational models.

E-BUSINESS MODELS

Cases

Harvard professor Lynda M. Applegate is an acknowledged expert on the leading edge of e-business models. She has published extensively on the impact of information technologies on organizational models, structures, and strategies, with 100 cases and articles available online at Harvard Business School Publishing (www.hbsp.harvard.edu). Recent cases include the 16-year transformation of the Port of Singapore into global e-business Portnet.com, B2C e-commerce company Submarino.com (with a presence in Brazil, Argentina, Mexico, Spain, and Portugal), Amazon.com, Medtronic, QuickenInsurance, and many others.

Interviews

Meta-group Consulting of Stamford, Connecticut offers online "Meta-Views" – brief (ten-minute) audio interviews on topics related to e-business. Each interview is accompanied by several graphic slides that visually express key concepts from the interview. Topics cover CCM, CRM, HCM, and OE (commerce chain management, customer relationship management, human capital management, and operations excellence), among others. Acronym interpreter sold separately (just kidding – and not needed on this helpful site). Of particular interest related to organizational models is the interview on *Creating E-Enterprises, or Click-and-Mortars* featuring Peter Burris, president and CEO of Metagroup.com, and Faisal Hoque, chairman and CEO of enamics, inc. (www.metagroup.com/metaview/mv0342/mv0342. html#links). Access is free.

Models

Business 2.0 (www.business2.com/webguide) is a comprehensive portal for up-to-the-minute Web-based business knowledge resources. Topic headings include Business, Careers, E-business, E-commerce, E-Learning, Finance, Industries, International, Internet, Management, Marketing, Networks, People, Security, Technology, and others. Each topic has multiple sub-headings linked to extensive, focused business links. For example, there are 19 links under Business Webs alone. Each sub-category is also cross-referenced, so the Web guide at the top provides links to people and case companies associated with that particular topic. You'll want to bookmark this site as an outstanding business portal.

One of the Business 2.0 b-webs topic links brings you to Bowstreet, Inc., an e-business solutions provider that automates the design and assembly of composite Web applications – key to facilitating the rapid proliferation of b-webs. Bowstreet promotes use and re-use of components across related families of applications, thereby enabling greater efficiency in successive development efforts. This dynamic site offers a globally-popular, bi-weekly, Webcast video seminar, with access to archives of prior seminars. Other resources include definitions, an extensive glossary of related terminology, white papers, monthly columns, a business Web service directory, and information on industry standards and FAQs (for resources go directly to www.bowstreet.com/resources).

Tapscott, D., Ticoll, D. & Lowy, A. (2000) *Digital Capital*, Harvard Business School Press. At the Website of Digital4Sight, which is the authors' consulting firm, you can download the first chapter of *Digital Capital*. The site also gives Tapscott's definition of b-web and the five different b-web types that the authors identify: Agora, Aggregation, Value Chain, Alliance, and Distributive Network (www.digital4sight.com).

Online courses

Crafting e-business models. Harvard Business School Publishing is expanding its own e-business model with the introduction of eLearning programs for sale on its Website (www.hbsp.harvard.edu). Of particular interest regarding organizational models is *Crafting e-business models*, a module taught by Professor Lynda M. Applegate (see above). Based on extensive applied research, the program features 17 emerging e-business models that include aggregators, marketplaces, exchanges, and portals. An interactive case study is used, and interviews with industry experts and executives are provided to help illustrate the concepts presented in the course. The program is designed to help users differentiate among different e-business models and choose the most appropriate model(s) to fit their particular circumstances.

The cost is $195 for the two-hour program, which includes one year of unlimited access via Internet. Order at www.hbsp.harvard.edu/hbsp/prod_detail.asp?5238M1

Free online course – Managing the digital enterprise. This outstanding resource is the work of Professor Michael Rappa, the Ian T. Dickson Distinguished University Professor of Technology Management at North Carolina State University in Raleigh, and formerly professor at MIT. Rappa specializes in the study of e-commerce and the assessment of emerging technologies. The course is an "open courseware" project (digitalenterprise.org/index.html) begun in 1998, and is based on the following principles: the course is open all the time, everywhere, and to everyone, free of charge. It is open-minded, open to collaboration and constant change, and based on open architecture. It is currently used by more than 150 universities world-wide as a resource in teaching e-commerce, as well as by several corporations for their in-house programs. It was the first course of its kind to adopt an open courseware approach based entirely on Web content.

Course topics include: an introduction, navigating the Web, digital design, Web metrics, business models (digitalenterprise.org/models/models.html), digital markets, agents, auctions, channel conflict, trust in cyberspace, security and encryption, privacy, intellectual property, governance, and Web ethics. Each week's topic is structured in the same way and includes links to readings, Websites, current news articles, radio stories, Webcast lectures by leading experts on the topic, additional links, questions to ponder, and things to review. Estimated time commitment (outside of class for on-campus students) is six hours per week, but each topic may be accessed independently as a rich learning resource. You may follow the entire course or only the segments that most interest you. The course can be found at digitalenterprise.org with the business model segment of the course is located at digitalenterprise.org/models/models.html

White papers

Consulting firms, research firms, and think tanks produce white papers on various topics related to information technology, including e-business models, and Yahoo! and Bitpipe have partnered to create an online marketplace for these research and knowledge papers (yahoo.bitpipe.com). Users can sign up to be notified by e-mail when new white papers on selected topics are published. Some are available online for free, while others require a substantial investment (e.g., $1500). Here are links to several free papers related to e-business models.

Defining the e-business model – A Tanning Technology White Paper, by Bipin Agarwal, July 23, 2001, Tanning Technology Corporation (www.tanning.com). This site provides an overview of the e-business phenomenon, and defines a model for successful e-business which involves an integration of three domains – strategies, business processes, and knowledge management. It can be found at yahoo.bitpipe.com/data/detail?id=995883778_166&type=RES&x =908731749

Services maturity model. A systematic approach to managing your services business, by QuickArrow, Inc (www.quickarrow.com), September 17, 2001. This paper explores choosing the right business model for professional services organizations from among three possibilities: transactional, operational, and systematic. (yahoo.bitpipe.com/data/detail?id=1001007315_995& type=RES&x=2062661086)

Mobile Internet – changing business models: billing for content, by Nathan Rae, Lucent Technologies Inc. (www.lucent.com), May 1, 2001. Explores the impact of the dawning age of mobile Internet on current mobile operators (i.e., cellphone providers), and provides a model for revenue generation based on the successful innovations of a Japanese company, NTT DoCoMo. (yahoo.bitpipe.com/data/ detail?id=992974030_618&type=RES&x=381951389)

A broader range of highly targeted white papers will undoubtedly become available as research, consulting, and business services firms increasingly market their capabilities on the Web.

OTHER ORGANIZATIONAL MODELS

Boundaryless organization

Ashkenas, R. (1999) "Creating the boundaryless organization (innovations in business management)." *Business Horizons*, September.

This in-depth article provides a helpful overview of the need for and characteristics of this model. The article is adapted by author Ron Ashkenas from his book, *The Boundaryless Organization*, co-authored with Dave Ulrich, C.K. Prahalad, and Todd Jick (Jossey-Bass, San Francisco 1995), which was reissued in soft cover in 1998, together with a workbook, *The Boundaryless Organization Field Guide.*

Chaordic commons

www.chaordic.org provides information and resources on the nature of chaordic systems, with a library of materials that includes definitions, characteristics, an overview of the pilot projects in chaordic organizing, articles, speeches, a reading list, and more. The site also provides information and materials on becoming an owning member of the organization, and on activities and workshops on creating chaordic organizations.

Hollow organization

Werther, W.B.Jr, (1999) "Structure-driven strategy and virtual organization design." *Business Horizons*, March/April. In this article, Werther states, "As used here, the difference between 'hollow' and 'virtual' organizations is one of intent and extent. Hollow firms seek economies within the current structure; virtual firms externalize all but core activities. Thus, virtual firms may be little more than a shell, performing only one or two key functions and not much more." The full article gives the example of Chrysler's successful "hollowing out" process (www.findarticles.com/cf_0/m1038/2_42/54370811/print.jhtml).

Matrix organization

A quick search on Yahoo.com yields 2300 hits, evidence of the continuing popular use of this model. Strategic Futures Consulting Group, Inc. provides training and consultation to government agencies. The Website www.strategicfutures.com/library.htm offers a library of helpful resources, including two practical articles on matrix organization by Ronald A. Gunn: "Matrix management: method, not magic," and "Five not so easy pieces of matrix management." The library also offers articles on cross-functional and virtual teams, among other topics.

The Concurrent Engineering Website differentiates among several possible organizational structures for managing projects, ranging from functional to "light" and "heavy" forms of matrix, to project organization. Graphic images are used to help illustrate the concepts in the accompanying text (www.tm.tue.nl/race/ce/org_pl5.html).

Organizational structure and design

This is a section of an excellent online course and hyperlinked book (*Supervision*) provided by Professor Gemmy Allen of the Business and Technology Division at Mountain View College in Dallas, Texas. The materials have also been used by a variety of corporate clients. The site provides graphics and text on organizational models, including functional, divisional, matrix, and boundaryless structures, as well as information on elements of organizational structure including formalization and centralization, and much more (ollie.dcccd.edu/mgmt1374/book_contents/3organizing/org_process/org_process.htm).

Shamrock organization

Jo Ann Klein, MS, RN-C provides an in-depth review of Charles Handy's 1989 book, *The Age of Unreason* (Harvard Business School Press, Boston, 1989), in which Handy describes the characteristics of this three-leaved organizational metaphor (www.nursingnetwork.com/orgstruc.htm).

Virtual organization

VoNet (Virtual Organization Net) was founded in 1996 as a platform for discussion about the upcoming topic of virtual organizations. A quarterly newsletter was published with articles from researchers from all over the world. The first International Workshop on Organizational Virtualness took place in Bern, Switzerland, in Spring 1998, and the second took place in Zurich the following year. This led to the creation of the *Electronic Journal of Organizational Virtualness* in Spring 1999. The Website offers access to academic journal articles on virtual organization, an online forum, news service, list of related definitions, resource links, and more (www.virtual-organization.net).

Brint.com provides extensive links to research, books, and articles on virtual organizations and new organizational forms, with a separate set of links on outsourcing. One could easily lose oneself here for a while with the wealth of resources available (www.brint.com/EmergOrg.htm)

Relatively brief, helpful articles on virtual organizations may also be found at:

» www.yeack.com/cyberlib/on/21ST_CEN/virtual.htm
» www.pscw.uva.nl/is/js/virt/hst1.htm

Ten Steps to Effective Organizational Models

Should you change your organizational model? Possibly. But before you do, carefully consider the need for change, the risks inherent in the change process, the psychological nature of organizational models, and ways to manage the change process successfully.

» Changing models: hidden dangers.
» As within, so without: if not ... watch out!
» Ten steps to effective organizational models.

By now you may be eager to re-invent your own organization and implement a snazzy new model, and hopefully one *not* based on autocracy, psychic prisons, or instruments of domination (if you missed those models the first time around, don't go back to search for them now!) But before you embark on a bold model-changing expedition, be forewarned: danger ahead; you may be skating on thin ice. This chapter provides insight into some of the risks inherent in changing models, as well as some ways to navigate the change process successfully. It concludes with ten guidelines for working effectively with organizational models.

CHANGING MODELS: HIDDEN DANGERS

You may at this point feel woefully out of step with the times and eager to scrap whatever facsimile of an organizational model you've been laboring under for a more glamorous version in tune with nature, silicon, and the new millennium. Should you hurry off to do so? Perhaps. However, before you race off towards transformation, you may want to familiarize yourself with some dangers that lie hidden in the murky waters of model-changing – particularly in a high-tech start-up environment – in order to avoid potentially needless loss of revenue and key personnel.

In a recent study,[1] James Burton and Michael Hannon of Stanford, with Diane Burton of MIT, studied the impact of changing organizational models on employee turnover and revenue generation in 173 Silicon Valley high-tech start-ups between 1991 and 1994. Based on initial interviews with organizational founders, they developed five distinct types of models (yes, more models) in use, which varied along three primary dimensions.

» **Attachment**, which refers to three primary means of motivating employees to work for a company: interesting and challenging work; monetary exchange; or intense emotional, often family-like bonds.
» **Means of co-ordinating and controlling work**, either informally through peers, professionally through socialization, formally through systems and procedures, or directly through oversight.
» **Methods for personnel selection**, based on skills, cultural fit, or long-term potential.

These three dimensions clustered into five unique models.

1 **Star** – just like it sounds, the model is based on hiring star talent with long-term potential, drawn by challenging work and control via professionalism (a variation on Professional Bureaucracy, see Chapter 3; also note that this is a second model called Star, not to be confused with its namesake described in Chapter 8 which is named after its shape, not its talent).

2 **Engineering** – the predominant model among high-tech Silicon Valley start-ups, based on challenging work, peer group control, and skills-based selection practices (also similar to Professional Bureaucracy, see Chapter 3).

3 **Commitment** – to family-like bonds with the organization, selection based on cultural fit, and peer group control (similar to Family Model, see Chapter 3).

4 **Bureaucracy** – just in case you thought it didn't exist in high-tech start-ups! By now, of course, you've guessed that control is through formal systems and procedures, selection based on skills and abilities, and attachment is via challenging work more than love or money (see Chapter 3).

5 **Autocracy** – me boss, you work, me pay. Money motivates; boss oversees work closely and directly, and hires for specifically pre-defined tasks (similar to Mintzberg's Simple Structure, see Chapter 3).

RESEARCH FINDINGS

Knowledge workers are the primary resource in high-tech start-ups. Therefore, turnover has the potential of being extremely disruptive, if not fatal, to young high-tech firms. Significantly, changing a company's founding model was found to increase significantly the turnover of its employees and to decrease significantly its ability to boost revenues – a vital measure of performance in young, growing technology companies.

Yet it appears that all changes of organizational models are not alike. There are substantial differences based on the particular models involved in a change. First, changing to a bureaucratic or autocratic model increased turnover, and changing from either of them to another model decreased turnover. Changing to bureaucracy from any other model increased turnover substantially. Yet bureaucracy yielded the *lowest* turnover rate of all of the models when it was a company's founding model and continued to remain in use by that company over time (i.e. no model change). Autocracy generated high turnover rates both as a company's founding model and as a company's change-to model.

The most disruptive effects were encountered when companies changed from either the star or commitment models, whereas any disruption due to changing from a bureaucratic model was apparently counterbalanced by employees' approval of the change, thereby resulting in lower turnover. Thus, "the benefit associated with shifting to a basic model type depends on the underlying attractiveness of that model" and "changing the premises governing employment relations disrupts an organization's equilibrium."[1] Just how disruptive seems to depend upon the desirability to employees of the model that the organization is changing to. "The commitment and star models appear to be particularly risky to dismantle and less contentious to adopt. In contrast, moving from bureaucracy and autocracy entails little disruption, whereas moving toward these models seems especially unsettling."[1]

Interestingly, the most pervasive model in the Silicon Valley, the engineering model, "appeared to be relatively more flexible and adaptable (i.e., easier to dismantle and easier to migrate to) than various other models ... The engineering model might have less upside but also less downside risk, compared to more fragile and distinctive models, such as the commitment or star blueprint, which entail greater potential returns *and* risks ... Hence, in some ecologies and for some strategies, adhering faithfully to a second-best (or even third-best) model might be superior to rapid oscillation among shorter-lived, first-best models."[1] Thus, for some organizations, the state of the art may involve sticking with a less-glamorous model and avoiding the compulsion to change.

Finally, the researchers ruled out a potential counter-argument: that changes in turnover were due to changes in leadership. Although they note that the findings may not apply to other industries, regions, or organizations, their ground-breaking research raises significant questions. It certainly suggests that all models are not alike, and sheds light on hidden dangers that may underlie changing one's organizational model.

AS WITHIN, SO WITHOUT: IF NOT ... WATCH OUT!

The seasoned manager will not be surprised that change – whether of organizational model or even of something as simple as office location – can engender resistance, turnover, and other unwelcome, deleterious consequences. Recall that organizational models are figments of our individual and collective imaginations. They may become built into systems, procedures, explicitly-expressed organizational missions, and values, etc., but they live, first and foremost, in the mind.

Managers who attempt to change their organization's model must pay close attention to the fact that all members of the organization carry within them a customized, generally unconscious mental model of that same organization, particularly in the form of an internalized "employment contract." Members develop these models in a variety of ways over time, and they – the models – are resilient to change. Once mental models have been developed, "people do not necessarily work hard on changing [them]. People work hard on fitting experiences into them,"[2] says Denise M. Rousseau, professor of Organizational Behavior at Carnegie Mellon University, and author of *Psychological Contracts in Organizations: Understanding Written and Unwritten Agreements.* "Because of discontinuous information processing," she says, "people often see what they expect to see, gather information only when they think they need it, and ignore a lot."[2]

Rousseau describes a continuum of psychological contracts that range from strictly transactional at one end of the spectrum to entirely relational at the other. Transactional contracts essentially revolve around market transactions, as in equitable work for equitable pay, whereas relational contracts involve high levels of interdependence and considerable investment in the relationship by both employers and employees. (Note that this continuum bears some resemblance to Powell's markets – networks – hierarchies continuum of interorganizational models described in the section *Organizational Collaboration* in Chapter 6).

After tracing the evolution of psychological contracts, Rousseau distinguishes four generic types of modern psychological contracts arranged along two dimensions: the intended duration of the relationship, and the degree of specification of the terms of performance. The four models are as follows.

1 **Transactional** – which describes short-term work arrangements with specified performance terms, as in seasonal sales clerks. This model typically involves high turnover and little ambiguity, commitment, integration into the organization, or learning. This model might apply to intermittent workers in a shamrock organization (see Chapter 8).

2 **Transitional** – also short-term but with unspecified performance terms, as experienced by employees in organizations following a merger or acquisition, or perhaps in the wake of the dot-com shakeout, or a significant change from one organizational strategy or model to one that is not yet clear. Uncertainty, ambiguity, and instability abound, with lots of folks "jumping ship." Not a pleasant place to be, and not sustainable for long. Rousseau points out that these transitions are typically away from relationally-based contracts (e.g., family model) and toward a transactional model.

3 **Relational** – is based on the expectancy of a longer-term relationship with unspecified performance terms, as with members of a family business. This model is characterized by high levels of member commitment, affective commitment, identification and integration with the organization, and stability. There is substantial, ongoing investment in the relationship by both employer and employees over time. This was the typical employment contract in nostalgic days of yore when environments and organizations were relatively stable over significant stretches of time.

4 **Balanced** – also based on a longer-term relationship but with specified performance terms, as with members of high-involvement teams. Like the relational model, this one is also characterized by high member commitment, integration, and identification, in a dynamic, mutually-supportive environment that fosters ongoing development of its people.

When managers try to change significantly or to replace a prevailing model that has been normalized in the organization (that is, embedded in its culture through the minds and behaviors of its members), members may experience it as a violation of their psychological contract with the organization, and may have a real sense of loss as a result. Members' responses to an experience of violation may be constructive or destructive, either actively or passively.

For managers, understanding the psychological dynamics of organizational transformation is key to making substantive changes to organizational models. Rousseau calls the process contract transformation, and distinguishes it from the experience of violation. "In transformation, an existing contract ends," she explains, "sometimes through breach, other times by completion, and a new contract is created. Losses are real and costs are high, but the gains may be too. Violation by definition is a wilful breach of contract that costs the person violated. There is often a fine line between violation and transformation ... The purpose of contract transformation is the creation of a new contract in place of an existing one, where the new contract engenders commitment and efficacy for all concerned. The process of transformation determines whether change degenerates into violation or transforms the basis of the relationship."[2]

There are actions that managers can take to help to ensure that the change leads to transformation, not violation. Rousseau offers ten steps for successfully managing the process.

1. Provide a clear, well-articulated rationale for the change, based on valid external circumstances.
2. Involve organizational members in gathering information on the external circumstances that necessitate the change.
3. Complete the past by acknowledging and even celebrating the old model or contract.
4. Meticulously assess the potential losses involved in the change, and then work diligently to minimize those losses as much as possible.
5. Build strong communication networks vertically and horizontally throughout the transition process. Implement interdisciplinary planning teams and frequent cross-level meetings.
6. People want more information and structure during times of uncertainty. Create interim practices and structures that involve short-term projects and activities that support the long-term objectives (e.g. training).
7. Manage the "meaning of change by expressing current efforts in terms of long-term objectives."[2]
8. Integrate change efforts into training and other human resource activities.

9 Create events to promote acceptance of the new model (e.g., orientation, internal recruiting).
10 Seek input from members on the effectiveness and thoroughness of the implementation of the new model. Take corrective action quickly when needed.

Even if there is a strong rationale for the change internally (for example, greater efficiency of internal processes), it may be resisted without providing valid external reasons for the change. For example, a "set of difficulties arose in the 1970s with the introduction of the matrix organization (Davis & Lawrence, 1977). Most of the reasons cited for shifting to a matrix form were internal, such as the need for managerial efficiency. The failure of organizations to adopt the theoretically more efficient matrix form may partly be due to the absence of externally-validated reasons for contract change. A turning point in organizational change efforts came with the Total Quality Movement of the 1980s. The widespread use of benchmarking made it more likely that organization members would look at the competition for knowledge about their organization's relative health and look to firms in unrelated industries for information on best practices and innovations."[2]

Much of this unfortunately reflects – by virtue of admonishments to "involve members," "manage meaning," etc. – the ongoing pervasiveness of models of organization that significantly constrain employee ownership, involvement, and voice. The end-result is that employee buy-in must be bought or coerced. "The truth is, an organization has no reality save in the mind," Dee Hock notes. "It is a mental construct – a concept to which people and resources are either drawn or compelled in pursuit of purpose. Every *healthy* organization is no more than a manifestation of a very old, very basic idea, the idea of community. Thus, the success of any healthy institution has infinitely more to do with clarity of shared purpose and principles, and strength of belief in them, than to all assets, technology, or management practices, important as they may be. To the direct degree that such shared beliefs exist, constructive, harmonious behavior is induced. To the direct degree they do not exist, behavior is inevitably compelled.

"It is not complicated. The alternative to shared belief in purpose and principles is tyranny. And tyranny, whether petty or grand, whether commercial, political, or social, is inevitably destructive. And, make no mistake about it, purpose and principles created at the top and mandated are not purpose and principles of the people which compose an organization, they are compulsion. It is from the sense of the members of each organizational community that deeply-held, shared purpose and principles must be evoked."[3]

It takes time, courage, and commitment, and maybe even a good dose of common sense, to create organizations as communities that honor and include all members. It is possible to change organizational models in ways that transform the organization and the relationships among its members for the benefit of all concerned – and that is key, *for the benefit of all*. Collaborative development of deeply-held, shared purpose and principles is at the heart of organizational communities that thrive. May you and yours thrive in the twenty-first century.

TEN STEPS TO EFFECTIVE ORGANIZATIONAL MODELS

We are finally ready to unveil the long-awaited, requisite ten steps. Of course, as the preceding chapters have illustrated, organizational models are wildly diverse and far-ranging. That diversity is likely to escalate in the future. Do not consider these steps as a blueprint, but rather as a palette of guidelines to draw upon when working with your own organizational models.

1 **Begin at the beginning**, and that doesn't mean go back to bureaucracy. Begin with what matters, with the heart and soul of the organization. Invest ample time in nurturing the development of shared purpose and principles, and then let the system organize itself in support of them. Soon you'll be able to toss out the policy manuals, if you haven't already, as your organizational members come to *embody the shared purpose and principles*. It is the key to success of so many organizational systems. Make it yours, too.

2 **Boldly imagine** – as you collectively develop your purpose and principles – the contribution that you'd like your organization to be in the world. Think beyond profits. It will do you good, and ignite the spirit of your people.

3 **Involve others** – right from the outset, and in full-voice, not simply as token advisers, or to rubber-stamp a decision you've already

made. Be sure to include the voices that are not often heard – and that have a stake in the result. Broaden the scope of participation as widely as possible. Keep in mind that participation is one of the primary approaches to effective implementation. After all, what good is a non-implemented model? Of course, if your organization is a worker democracy, you don't need to involve others. They are already involved.

4 **Organize to achieve purpose**, not structure. This is where strategy comes in. Little is said in this book about the role of strategy, as there are other books in this series and ample books elsewhere that address the subject in depth. But strategy without purpose is incomplete. Begin with purpose, then develop strategies that support its manifestation.

5 **Structure to achieve purpose**. Ideally, form should follow function, and structure should result from and be developed in support of purpose and strategy – not just to mimic the most dazzling model of the month. Make sure your model is right for your people and your purpose.

6 **Consider disaggregating non-core functions** if you haven't already. New technologies are significantly enabling truly virtual organizations and yielding big rewards. Use technologies to maximum advantage.

7 **Get to know your model**. Even if you are not creating or changing your organizational model, knowing the model that you are working with and in can do wonders for your effectiveness. Suddenly the whole organization may make sense to you in way that it hasn't before.

8 **Get to know others' models**. You'll see them in the business press. They may not say *organizational model* on them, but you'll begin to recognize models when you see them. Expand your thinking. Models are figments of our imagination. Stretch yours, and you might envision a whole new possibility, or two or three.

9 **Evolve your model** out of purpose and principles. Don't destroy and reconstruct. As Dee Hock says, "that's madness." Models are not things, they are ideas. Do it the way nature does it, and your bureaucracy may morph into a shamrock or a star.

10 **Whatever you do, keep in mind that organizations do not exist.** Organizations are figments of our individual and collective imaginations. Develop a healthy respect and appreciation for the fact that every person in your organization holds a somewhat resilient organizational model in their brain. Model-changing involves transforming those internal images of organization, not just external structures. Keep this in mind, and ensure that everyone else does so too. See Rousseau's ten steps for managing that process (above).

KEY LEARNING POINTS

» In Silicon Valley high-tech start-ups:
  » changing to a bureaucratic or autocratic model increased turnover;
  » but bureaucracy had the *lowest* turnover rate among models when there was no change in model;
  » for some organizations, it may be better to stay with a less glamorous model and avoid the compulsion to change.
» Psychological contracts include transactional, transitional, relational, and balanced.
» The process of changing models may transform the organization and relationships among its members, or it may cause members to feel violated. It depends on how the process is managed.
» Shared purpose and principles must be evoked from the members of the organizational community, not mandated from the top down.

NOTES

1 Baron, J.N., Hannan, M.T., & Burton, M.D. (2001) "Labor pains: change in organizational models and employee turnover in young, high-tech firms." *American Journal of Sociology*, January.
2 Rousseau, D.M. (1995) *Psychological Contracts in Organizations: Understanding Written and Unwritten Agreements*. Sage Publications, Inc., Thousand Oaks, CA.

3 Hock, D.W. (1998) "An epidemic of institutional failure." Keynote Address, Organization Development Network Annual Conference, New Orleans, LA, November 16 Full text available online at www. ODNetwork.org/confgallery/deehock.html

Frequently Asked Questions (FAQs)

Q1: How are "organizational model" and "business model" defined?

A: See Chapter 2, the section *Basic definitions*.

Q2: How is a business model related to an organizational model?

A: See Chapter 2, the section *Basic definitions*, and Chapter 3, the section entitled *From organizational models to business models*.

Q3: Is bureaucracy really dead?

A: See Chapter 6, the section *Bureaucracy: dead, dying, or immortal?*

Q4: What are some of the key organizational models?

A: The diversity of organizational models is explored throughout this book. In particular, see Chapter 3, the section entitled *Organizational models of the twentieth century*; Chapters 4, 5, and 6; Chapter 8, *Even more models and metaphors*; and Chapter 9, *Other organizational models*.

Q5: In what ways do national cultures influence models of organization?

A: See Chapter 5, the section entitled *The impact of culture*.

Q6: What impact is the Internet having on organizational models?

A: See Chapter 4, the section *Business webs*; and the first two success stories presented in Chapter 7.

Q7: Is there a viable alternative to the shareholder model?

A: See the discussion related to the founding of VISA under *The future of organizational collaboration* in Chapter 6; and the final success story presented in Chapter 7, *Incubating worker democracies: the Mondragon model*.

Q8: What is a "business web?"

A: See Chapter 4, the section on *Business webs*; and the first two success stories in Chapter 7 for illustrations of business webs.

Q9: How do we change our organizational model?

A: Begin with *Changing models: hidden dangers*, followed by *As within, so without: if not . . . watch out!* in Chapter 10.

Q10: Where can I find some of the best information and resources on business and organizational models online?

A: See Chapter 9, *Resources for Organizational Models*.

Acknowledgments

Writing a book is a daunting and exciting challenge. THANK YOU to everyone who helped make it possible:

» Capstone Publishing Limited and Suntop Media – for providing the opportunity;
» Stuart Crainer and Des Dearlove – for their faith in me, patience, and ongoing encouragement;
» Tom Fryer of Sparks Computer Solutions Ltd – for neatly expediting the process from first draft to press;
» Roger Witts – for his care in copy-editing;
» Tom Brown – for seeing the writer in me and encouraging me to unleash it;
» Ken Murrell – for being such a great, empowering mentor;
» Janis Fitzgerald – for her enthusiasm and emotional support;
» Richard Clark – for encouraging me to write, and keep it simple;
» All of the interviewees – for their responsiveness, flexibility, insight, and inspiration;
» All of the business thinkers and researchers who contribute to our understanding of organizational and business models;
» And especially to all those who strive to create models of organization that not only thrive economically, but that are socially and environmentally sustainable, and that liberate the human spirit.

Index

Printed and bound by CPI Group (UK) Ltd, Croydon, CR0 4YY

13/04/2025

14656564-0002